We Never Left the Garden

Pamela Galadrial

Mount Tallac Press
South Lake Tahoe, CA

We Never Left the Garden

Pamela Galadrial

Mount Tallac Press
South Lake Tahoe, CA 96152

Requests for such permission should be addressed to:
    Mount Tallac Press
    P.O. Box 612300
    So. Lake Tahoe, CA 96152

ISBN: 0-9647585-1-2

Library of Congress Catalog Card Number 95-94950

Painting on cover entitled *In the Beginning* oil on canvas, 36 x 48, 1992, by Dario Campanile

Illustrations by Margot Gresham

Cover and Text design by Mary Guido

The ideas represented herein are the personal interpretation and understanding of the author and are not endorsed by the copyright holder of a *A Course in Miracles*©

Printed in the United States of America

Contents

$Preface$

Have you ever wanted to do something, not knowing where or how to begin? For several years I have felt guided to write a book. I even started one 5 years ago, but thoughts would always arise: "I don't know how," "It's all been written." So no book!

Then I went on the road, conducting playshops (I prefer "play" over "work"!), performing concerts, and selling tapes of my music. Time after time at these events someone would ask me how they could obtain a copy of my book, and I would find myself saying "I haven't written it yet." Sometimes I wonder what it will take for the Universe to get my attention.

So today I begin. I know that this book will be different than the one I started five years ago, because I am different. If there is one constant in life it is change, and if I wait another five years, that too would be a different book. Does that mean I shouldn't write this book? No. How often do we find ourselves choosing to postpone joy?

A large part of me understands that this book is actually for me. It is a part of my journey, my process. If it touches you, then we have joined together and I believe a healing has occurred, for whenever two or more are joined together in understanding, or in love, change happens and we move together towards our goal of being free and remembering that we are whole. Notice that I did not say "we *move toward* becoming whole." I believe we are *already* whole. We have simply forgotten this fact and have chosen to play different roles in this drama called life. Some of these roles look extremely painful, and on the physical plane they are: one person may seem blessed while another isn't; one person may appear to be a monster while another seems to be a victim. These are simply roles through which we learn, however.

For me this is a time of discovery — finding the obstacles to freedom, joy, and peace, releasing these obstacles and then moving beyond my comfort zones* to explore new ways of seeing things and creating healthy behavior patterns. It is a trial and error process. I heard Buckminister Fuller state that "As humans we need to stop blaming ourselves for making mistakes, because it is through our mistakes we learn." Hopefully in the near future we will love ourselves enough to learn from others' mistakes. We will learn through observing the painful mistakes others make, so we will not need to repeat them. Until then, we need to be gentle with ourselves. We need to focus on our successes, rather than our seeming failures. We need to recognize the progress we have made, rather than how much further we think we have to go. Arnold Patent, author of *You Can Have It All* teaches a "Universal Principle" that what we focus on, expands. If we want to remember the truth of who we are, focus on truth rather than fantasy, love rather than fear, and forgiveness rather than judgment. These are the keys to freedom.

I once wrote a song entitled "Beings of Light" which expresses the belief that each human being is a being of light. Quantum physics seems to be proving that this idea has a strong basis in reality. If we are to remember this truth about ourselves—that we are in fact Beings of Light—we need to start "lightening up" and stop taking ourselves so seriously. In releasing our heavy burdens of guilt, fear and judgment

---

* Have you ever wondered why we call our painful, compulsive patterns "comfort zones?"

we automatically move into a different rate of vibration with our thoughts as well as in our physical and emotional bodies. We literally "lighten up."

So this book is a "How to" book: how to live from a conscious state of love; how to move beyond the paralyzing emotions of fear, guilt, and judgment and move into a place of freedom to be the You you were meant to be. Perhaps we'll both laugh and cry together. We'll learn to take each other and ourselves lightly. Chuck C. put it so beautifully in the title of his book: we'll put on "*A New Pair of Glasses.*"

One other thought I would like to touch upon in this introduction is the concept of gratitude. There is a well known slogan in 12-step groups that encourages us to live "an attitude of gratitude." I will expand on this later in the book. For now I want to express my gratitude to all the people in my life who have helped me become the person I am today. That really means I wish to thank everyone who has touched my life in some way or another, for every event in my life has helped me to be the person I am today, with the understanding, peace and joy that I now experience. Everyone in my life has been my teacher. Just to name a few: thank you Mom and Dad, Ronnie, Patrick, Jeff, Scott, Richard, Arnold and Selma Patent, Tom and Linda Carpenter, Patricia Remele, Judy, Phillip, Marge, Peter, Jonathan, Jerry, Julie, Jack and Cheryl, Paul and Bobbie and the San Diego company of Playback Theater. It is interesting to note that included in this list are the people who brought me the greatest challenges in my life up to this point. Our greatest teachers can be those who assist us in becoming aware of our hidden blocks to love's awareness.

The purpose of this book

The purpose of this book is to identify and remove our blocks to love's awareness, thereby remembering the truth about ourselves and each other.

The form of this book

This book will include many different forms. It will be a combination of direct guidance that I have received, stories from my life, talks I have given, guided meditations for the reader, lots of metaphors, and, of course, my understanding of the teachings I have studied, most importantly *A Course in Miracles*. My hope is that this book will be amusing as well as informative, inspirational as well as educational, and, most of all, that it brings you to the point of finding your own truth—which can only be found within.

About God

What is God? Throughout my travels and studies, God has appeared in many different forms and a variety of ideas and speculations, most of which reflect a God made in the image and likeness of man. Your God may not be the same as your neighbors' or even your parents'. In fact, you may not even believe in God. Many of us continue to have a very negative reaction to the word "God" as a result of the programming we received as children concerning this all powerful, judgmental force.

There are numerous names for God: Father, Mother/Father, Higher Power, Holy Spirit, Yahweh, Universal Mind, Infinite Intelligence, and many, many more. The God of my understanding has changed throughout my life. As a Roman Catholic I was taught about an all powerful God who loved but also judged, it was a God to respect and fear. In my twenties, I abandoned thoughts about and association with *any* God. In my thirties, I began to re-embrace God, but this God was more of a "quantum physics God." My God is a force: an all-pervasive energy, always and ever present, supporting and interacting with all of us; we are a part of this force. This God may be beyond our current level of understanding, but Its essence is that of pure love, peace and unbounded joy. For me, God has become more of a feeling, rather than an idea. It may appear to us that very little of the true essence of this Force is reflected here today on our planet, although we experience sparks of It upon occasion. Hopefully the following journey will help you to connect with your own understanding of what God is in your life. The journey is a challenging yet simple one, culminating in truth, peace and joy.

I have been tempted not to use the word God in this book, so as not to offend a portion of the reading public. But the question kept arising: how do we heal our relationship with this force if I ignore It? After all, the purpose of this book is to identify and remove the blocks we have to the awareness of love. I will be using a variety of words to talk about this Force, therefore, such as Higher Power, True Self, Infinite Intelligence, Universal Intelligence, and God.

If you are unsure of what God is, or even if there is a God, do not be discouraged. As we open to accepting and loving ourselves, we will find our own inner truths. This book is a journey to self- acceptance and love. As we accept ourselves and each other with unconditional positive regard, we will find our relationship with a God of our own understanding.

1

$\mathcal{A}$ Metaphor

"Where we came from"

Once upon a time, a very long time ago (at least that is how it feels), you and I knew who and what we are: the perfect extension of God's love. We existed in a state of pure joy and perfect bliss. All we knew was unconditional love, and we were capable of nothing more. We knew that we were perfect. There was no separation, no time, no fear, no guilt, and no pain of any kind. We lived in a state of absolute harmony.

One "day" one of the children of God thought "How would it feel to be like Mom and Dad? What would it be like to leave home and create my own world?" This child decided to "run away from home" and live her life as she wanted. She walked up the long stairway to her room, took out her little suitcase, and packed it with a few of her favorite belongings. Then she went downstairs and outside into the very large backyard. She crossed the patio and went to the lawn area where Dad had built a beautiful tree house. She climbed up into the tree house and declared: "There, I've done it, I've run away from home and now I am free to play just like Mom and Dad."

Day turned to night and dark clouds filled the sky. The child could still see the house until it started to rain. Thunder and lightning were right above her. She suddenly began to feel different. She wondered if Dad and Mom knew where she was. Would they be angry when they realized she had run away from home? She began to feel something she had never felt before: guilt. And, because she felt this new feeling, she started to question her decision about leaving home. She soon felt another new sensation: fear. The longer she stayed out in the tree house, the more fear she felt. She began to believe that she would be severely punished when she did go home. So she stayed out in the tree house, afraid to come in from the rain.

In the meantime, Mother/Father God looked out from the main house to the tree house, knowing that their child was safe, having chosen to sleep outside that night. They did not know that the child was starting to experience new feelings. They only knew that she was safe and sound in the backyard.

This metaphor, given to me recently during a meditation, explains the dilemma that each of us feels at the core of our humanity. We are that little child still hiding out in that tree house, afraid to return home. We still think the rain is pouring down, and we have come to believe that we now live in a dangerous and fear-filled place. We call it Planet Earth. We also believe that we will indeed be punished if we return home (some call that Heaven), so we stay just outside the awareness of God, hiding. We also punish ourselves in many creative ways, because we believe that if we punish ourselves for a long enough time, and in enough pain-filled ways, we will somehow mitigate the punishment of God. (The Bible is filled with such stories). The truth is that we are still at home, but we don't quite see it that way.

I remember the first time I heard the idea that we are afraid of God. My first reaction was "how silly!" Why would anyone be afraid of God if God is absolute good? It didn't take me long to reflect on my own childhood, with my experiences of Catholicism and both the Old and New Testaments in the Bible, to realize just how afraid of God we really are. I grew up with the message that God so loved the world (us) that He crucified His only begotten son on a cross. Why wouldn't we be afraid of a God like that—a God who demands sacrifice and pain? Time after time in the Old Testament we read stories about God threatening punishment and then following through with these threats. Sodom and Gomorra is just one very picturesque example. Is it any wonder that we grow up fearing God, often rejecting God's very existence? We also received the message that this God is all-powerful, all-knowing and everywhere present. If you think about it, what could be more fearful than having this all-powerful Being mad at you? Imagine the kind of punishment such a Being could dispense!

I finally asked myself where and how these stories about a "Just and Fearful God" originated. Why did mankind feel the need to see its Creator as such an angry God? Why did man choose to live under the threat of annihilation by a Heavenly Creator? *A Course in Miracles* came to my rescue. There are many paths out there, and I trust that all of them lead home, but not all of them answer my questions. That book did. I was taught as a child that the truth was unavailable to me, and put in the category of "Mysteries," and available only to a privileged few. This seems to me a bit controlling—it certainly would keep the majority of us in the dark as well as in fear. (An excellent way for religious leaders to keep the masses under control, don't you think?) *A Course in Miracles* explains quite clearly that in the instant we made a decision to separate from God, we felt guilty, like the child in the metaphor. We believe that we left our happy home (remember the Adam and Eve story?), and that we turned our backs on God. This is a tremendous burden for us to bear. We chose to feel guilty, and that choice has been the cause of **ALL** of our problems.

Just imagine for a moment a world where everyone feels a sense of guilt at the base of his and her humanity. What would that look like? People would be afraid to be vulnerable, afraid to show their true feelings, afraid to be honest, because of their belief that they are not good enough. People would feel flawed, hiding from themselves and from others. They might try to protect their material possessions as a result of low self-esteem for fear they would lose what they had because they actually did not deserve it. They would begin to perceive differences amongst themselves, and for protection they would make laws and create boundaries (countries), creating even more camps (religious beliefs, nationalities etc.) There would be wars, famine, rich versus poor, famous versus infamous, and so on. Does this sound familiar? Remember, all this stems from one decision: the decision to feel guilt.

Okay, so here we are on Planet Earth at the end of the 20th century. We have created and live in a world based on guilt. We need only to pick up the morning newspaper or turn on the six o'clock news to see the results. How do we change it?

Quite simply, we change our minds about ourselves. All the rest will follow. We need to accept responsibility for the mess that we created. We need to understand how through our thoughts and judgments we continue to re-create the world the way it currently appears. We need to discover our individual parts, as well as our group efforts, our patterns, and our guilt-ridden habits so that we can consciously choose to change these patterns and habits.

At this point in time I wish to caution you not to become discouraged or pessimistic. One might easily be dismayed after the many thousands of years of destruction on this planet. When one first discovers that we all had a part in creating the mess the planet is in now, one could automatically choose to feel even more guilt. This is not helpful. What we need to do is *stop* feeling guilty. That is the major decision we need to make. Do not underestimate the power that *you* have to change the world when you make this decision!

Where do we begin? First, we need to understand and accept that this is a world where everyone does feel guilt. Next, when we accept that each of us does feel guilt, we need to look at what we try to do with this guilt. Naturally, we attempt to unload this burden, to give the guilt away. It doesn't really matter to whom, just so long as we think we can rid ourselves of it.

This has become a major pastime for us, and is one of our basic destructive patterns. No one wants to feel guilt. Guilt does not feel good. The question unconsciously became, "How do I unload this feeling of guilt?" I will give the guilt away! Since by giving the guilt away, one is no longer burdened by it. That makes sense from a human point of view. If I give away a piece of jewelry, or a car, or some old clothes, I don't have them anymore. Doesn't it work that way with guilt? Unfortunately, no. Instead of releasing the guilt by a simple choice of no longer *needing* to feel guilt, one still feels a need for this guilt at some level. One can only attempt to get rid of it by giving it to someone else. The logic becomes, "if I can make you feel guilty, I believe I will feel better." This usually works for a short period of time, but not for long. As a matter of fact, the process actually backfires. The guilt eventually resurfaces, because by giving it to you, I did not release my own guilt. In fact I increased it, since in addition to the old guilt I now feel guilty for making *you* feel guilty.

The pattern becomes one of projection. I give away my guilt to you by making you wrong, or bad, or guilty about something. I then feel free of guilt for a brief period of time, but soon I feel even more guilty because of what I perceive I did to you.

We can see this in all levels of our society: countries do it with countries, religious groups with religious groups, corporations with corporations, friends with friends, husbands and wives with each other, parents with children and vice versa. We all make each other wrong—which somehow is supposed to make us feel right. But all this does is perpetuate and strengthen the pattern, so that we all feel more and more separate from each other and at the same time increasingly separate from our Source: God, Love, Joy, Higher Power, or whatever your word for the "I AM" is.

I see this today in the area of child abuse for example. Statistics show that the majority of child abusers were in fact abused when they were children. Every person that I have worked with who was abused as a child feels shame and guilt about having done something wrong, even though they do not know what it is. This is especially true with sexual abuse. As adults they attempt to rid themselves of this shame or guilt. For many, this is done through the process of therapy or support groups. For others though, it is done by attempting to give it away, and sometimes this happens exactly the way it happened to them: they become the abuser. It is obvious that this act does not rid a person of the feeling of guilt or shame; it only compounds it.

The buck has to stop somewhere. That is where you and I as individuals come in. We can stop this vicious cycle simply by not trying to project our guilt onto anyone else, by ceasing to make each other wrong. It is quite simple *and* it does take practice. This book will look at many of the patterns that we have created to camouflage this exchange of guilt and keep us feeling separate from one another and our Source. We will discover solutions and alternate patterns that will change our perception of each other, ourselves, and the world. It is an exciting and immensely rewarding journey.

If you don't quite understand the implications of all this, relax, be gentle with yourself, and know that this is a step-by-step process, each building upon the other. It will all be crystal clear in time and you will find yourself living in a different world and reality than you thought. You will find yourself living in a world based in love and joy, and not on guilt.

Let's begin.

2

The End of Sacrifice

When I was in my early thirties, I decided that it was time to get my body into shape. I had not exercised for many years and my muscle tone was not what it should have been. My new husband had friends who lifted weights and they looked pretty terrific, so I decided to join a gym and work out three times a week. It just so happened that lots of serious body builders worked out there, including a recent winner of the Mr. USA title. He started working out at the same time as me and offered to coach me, in return for my "spotting" for him. (For those of you are not familiar with the term, "spotting" means assisting a person who is lifting free weights). I must confess that the gym was very quiet during this particular time of the day. Picture a 105 lb. out-of-condition me spotting for a Mr. USA. It is really quite a funny thought.

The theme at this gym was "no pain = no gain." Mr. USA explained to me that the process of gently ripping (gently ripping??) one's muscles would result in them growing back stronger and bulkier, which seemed to be the aim of most of the men there. (Female body-building was not quite the thing then, or at least I wasn't aware of it.)

I for one didn't want to look bulky, so I would work out with less weight and more repetitions. Mr. USA, however, would push his body to the limits of its endurance and beyond, which looked and sounded painful, not to mention the pain on the following day when the resulting lactic acid waste stagnated in his muscles.

Weight-lifting could easily be used as a metaphor for life as we have chosen to live it thus far. We have chosen to believe that we gain through pain. This belief is mirrored back to us in almost every area of our lives, and it works! We can gain through pain. What is it that we think we gain? On a conscious level we believe we gain ideals such as freedom, knowledge, or success, and perhaps conquests such as wealth, health and beauty.

We can see this pattern clearly throughout our history. We left Europe to come to America for financial and religious freedom. We fought wars to gain freedom. I think we can agree that war is painful. Soon after establishing their own independence, many of our founding fathers were knee-deep in enslaving others who had been kidnapped from their home country of Africa. The U.S. army later involved itself by attempting to eradicate an entire race of peoples, the Native American. The African American and the Native American peoples are still trying to establish their freedom and rights to this day. It is ironic to look back and see that as many of our founding fathers were fighting for their own freedom they were actively enslaving others, who, in turn, had to fight for their freedom.

Today we still believe that the price of freedom is pain, and that this price insists upon a winner and a loser. We will find pain in any situation where there is a perceived winner and a perceived loser. The game plan we see played over and over again is based upon the belief that someone must lose for another to gain. *A Course in Miracles* tells us that this belief is at the base of every one of our problems:

" The Holy spirit offers you release from every problem that you think you have. They are the same to Him because each one, regardless of the form it seems to take, is a demand that someone suffer loss and make a sacrifice that you might gain." [1]

Sacrifice

The message that we have received over and over again from our parents, our teachers and our governing bodies, is that any gain—wealth, beauty, success, knowledge—entails a cost, and that this cost is pain or loss. We usually call this pain "sacrifice." As an example, during the presidential race between Bill Clinton and George Bush we heard Clinton tell us of the "sacrifices" we must make to "make America strong once again." During the early part of his administration Clinton talked of the sacrifices we must make to have a National Health Care Plan.

When we look closely at this "no pain=no gain" belief, we find that underneath this agreement lies the **principle of Sacrifice.** We have chosen to believe that unless we sacrifice one thing, we can't have something else. To have wealth, we sacrifice leisure, our health, our relationships or any combination of the above. The phrase "Work hard and then you die" quickly springs to mind.

To be "beautiful" we must dress to a certain code, be a certain weight, and, no matter what, we must look young. I recently watched the making of a music video. One of the vocalists had spent three hours getting her hair done, and the other lead singer said: "She will pay any price for beauty," a phrase by which some live. Again we have sacrificed—we have sacrificed our right to our uniqueness. We feel the need to conform to what is expected of us, no matter the cost. We are bombarded by this message: young children receive it from advertisements on TV; teens receive it from ads and peer pressure; and adults who are already "fully programmed" with this message continue to receive it, not only from ads and peer pressure, but also from their children.

People also sacrifice in relationships on a daily basis. Have you ever settled for less than what you wanted in relationship because *any* relationship was better than none? Have you ever sacrificed a part of yourself in a relationship? We often create relationships based on need, giving up our own needs in order to get something else, perhaps peace for sex, freedom for perceived financial security, chaos in place of loneliness. I hear stories every week at Al-Anon meetings of how people have sacrificed their self-worth to keep a marriage alive. Is sacrificing our self-worth really being "alive?"

Why? Why this intense desire for sacrifice? For it **is** intense, and it **must** be a desire because we continually choose sacrifice. Why do we insist that sacrifice be part of the equation in attaining some form of gain? It reminds me of my childhood and my study of the Old Testament, which taught sacrifice in a big way. As far back in the Old Testament as the story of Cain and Abel, we see sacrifices being offered to God: a part of the harvest, the best lamb. God asked Abraham to sacrifice his son, who was spared by an angel at the last moment. In the New Testament we have the ultimate sacrifice—the "only son of God" sacrificed himself on the cross for the sins of mankind. No wonder we believe in sacrifice. We believe at a very deep level that God demands it. But again I ask—why? What is the underlying belief that compels us to continue this practice?

To make sacred

When we look at the root of the word, we find that sacrifice comes from the Latin *to make sacred*. Not so long ago, the concept of sacrifice had a somewhat different connotation than it does now. Sacrifice was not considered a burden, but a privilege and an honor. It was included in most rituals and it was treated as an integral part of life. Sacrifice was inspired by the belief that we must die to our ego self (the body) in order to transcend into the God self that is our True self. This is how we become sacred. As Joseph Campbell says in the *Power of Myth:*

> *"We must die to the flesh to be reborn in the spirit. As we identify with the Spirit we die to the idea that we are the body and identify that the body is simply a vehicle, a carrier of the Spirit. That which dies is born. We must have death to have life."* [2]

This original concept of sacrifice has been taught to us over and over in different stories in the Bible. This belief has existed for thousands and thousands of years, as evidenced by stories from cultures around the world. For example, Mayans played a sort of basketball game in a very large arena. At the end of the game, the captain of the *winning* team was sacrificed (killed) by the captain of the losing team. It was a great honor to die of the ego and be reborn to the spirit. It was not a burden to give up one's life, which was seen as moving into Spirit—God. I believe that life was looked upon more as a game with this attitude, a game to play with excitement and vigor, not heavy responsibility.

In religion today we are taught to identify with Spirit and not the body, which is simply a carrier of Spirit. A woman shared in a recent class of mine that her teacher asked her what she wanted to be when she grew up. She was nine at the time. She responded "I want to be a martyr," which she felt sure was the highest and best thing that she could do with her life. I can think of a lot of people who have lived their lives playing out the role of the martyr without ever having had that as a professional goal. But all of this brings me again to the same question: why sacrifice? What kind of a God would demand sacrifice of Its beloved children? This must be a very judgmental and fearful God, which of course is how God is depicted in the Bible. But if God created us in the image and likeness of Itself, and God is love and perfection, what need is there for us to sacrifice? Would a loving God demand loss?

Both the old understanding of sacrifice and our current one rest upon belief that one must lose in order to gain. Today it feels as though we not only are sacrificing the body for the higher purpose of eternal life, we also are sacrificing our very souls for the sake of the needs and desires of the body.

Both the old and new concepts of sacrifice glorify and camouflage. They imply sacrifice is honorable and productive. Both insist on the sacrifice of one thing for another, a giving to get, which is just another one of the ego's games. Perhaps the old understanding of sacrifice was aligned with the principle of surrender, which says that I must surrender the beliefs that I currently hold about myself before I can remember the truth of who I am. That may be true, but I do not agree that God ever demanded sacrifice of me or anyone else.

What caused us to believe that sacrifice was necessary? Why did we feel the need to appease God? Could it be that we believe we are deserving of pain, and that sacrifice is our chosen means of experiencing it? Let us again go back to this book's initial metaphor. Here we are out in the tree house, afraid to go back inside. Why? Because, on some level, we believe that we have done something bad or wrong. We decided to play separate from God, and we don't go home for fear of being punished—perhaps like God punished Jesus? That doesn't really appeal to me—does it to you? Instead we punish ourselves, since that way maybe God won't. Instead of choosing to cross the lawn and the patio and walk back inside God's house (our house), we choose to feel pain. What we are actually doing is crucifying ourselves over and over again by choosing to remain separate from our loving Source. We also sacrifice whenever we choose to believe that we are separate from one another. We do this every time we believe that someone (including ourself) is not a perfect child of our Creator.

Scarcity

Let me ask you another question. Do you know anyone, including yourself, who does not believe in scarcity in at least one area of their lives? I was taught scarcity in many ways as a child. "Eat all the food on your plate. Think of the poor starving babies in China." This statement implies not only that there is not enough food to go around, but that I need to eat all my food or feel guilty because I have food and another does not. The implication is that a child in China is sacrificing for my abundance. My first husband told me never to buy anything in the supermarket unless it was on sale, especially meat. There wasn't enough money for prime cuts of meat. I live in California and conserved water for seven years due to a lack of rain. Some scientists say we will not have sufficient air on the planet within 20 years.

We have a "lack consciousness," and we see it each and every day in hundreds of ways. Look at the National Debt— that is lack consciousness. We are now faced with a lack of landfill space for our refuse. That one really shows the absurdity of our belief. Underlying this belief in scarcity is the sacrifice principal: someone must lose for another to gain, only in this case we are focusing on how Mother Earth has sacrificed for the gain of mankind.

Although we are bombarded with the idea of lack and scarcity, the Universe in fact is absolute abundance, without lack of any kind. Our natural state is one of complete and total abundance, with all of our needs met before we even know what they are. Here in the plane of illusion, the tree house, we choose to see lack and limitation. We do an excellent job of making this seem extremely real. It only *seems* real however because we *believe* it is real, and it shows up that way in our "reality." Remember the oil shortage in the 80's? We would sit in lines at gasoline stations for hours. We believed that there was an oil shortage, when in fact there wasn't one. It was simply a great way to raise oil prices and to continue our belief in this silly game of sacrifice.

Okay, we see how we have chosen pain through sacrifice. How do we stop? We need to understand that God is not asking us to sacrifice. God is not asking us to feel pain or loss of any kind. It is our mistaken belief that we deserve pain that requires us to continue playing this insane game. It is our own sense of guilt that requires us to sacrifice, and that makes us believe that loss is possible. When we understand that the true nature of ourselves is absolute abundance, we will never again experience lack or limitation in any area of our lives, and sacrifice will look as meaningless as it really is.

It is impractical to believe that sacrifice is a requirement of God's love. First, God already loves us unconditionally. We need not and can not do anything to make God love us more. Absolute love is absolute love. Second, and much easier to recognize, is to learn from another person playing a sacrificial role. Think about someone in your life who played the victim. Did it inspire you to love them more, or to head for the hills? Sacrifice really doesn't work on any level. It is an exercise in futility, and a very painful one at that. *A Course in Miracles* tells us that

> " ...*there is but one mistake; the whole idea that loss is possible, and could result in gain for anyone.*" [3]

Sacrificing the Truth about Ourselves

In a broader context, we are sacrificing the Truth about ourselves. Anytime we say that sacrifice is necessary, we are reaffirming to ourselves and others that we are not who we really are: the perfect children of Source. We keep the game of illusion going through the practice of sacrifice. The only thing we need to sacrifice is the idea of sacrifice itself.

Sacrifice is impossible. There is never any loss in the Universe. There is only *perceived* loss. In other words, we only *think* we can lose something (that includes our own perfection). That very belief keeps us locked in the need to sacrifice though, because if we believe in the possibility of loss, we must also believe in the need to gain, and to gain someone must lose, and on and on in a vicious circle.

Continuing this practice is a waste of time and effort, because it doesn't work. We gain nothing. We think we have gained, but *all we do* is perpetuate the fallacy that someone else must lose in order for us to gain. Sacrifice will never work. It just keeps us feeling guilty, and needing to sacrifice more. Once we understand how insane this practice is, we can look at our own lives and discover where we are still acting on this belief. We need to stop glorifying it, stop camouflaging it and stop idealizing it. Only then can we stop doing it. Only when we let go of sacrifice can we let go of

our guilt. Only when we let go of our guilt can we give ourselves permission to walk from the tree house back into our
home, Heaven.

Let us choose to stop sacrificing now. Let us align ourselves
with the truth that (1) Sacrifice is impossible; (2) Sacrifice
doesn't work and doesn't endear us to anyone, including
God; and (3) the Universe is one of total abundance. We will
start experiencing abundance in our lives when we believe
this truth.

Exercises

1. Describe three areas of your life where you are aware
    that you are still sacrificing.

    1. _____

    2. _____

    3. _____

2. Describe what you are gaining in each of these situa-
    tions. What is the payoff for you? Examples: "I agree to
    do something I do not want to because I get recogni-
    tion for it." "I accept verbal abuse so that I do not have
    to stand up for myself. I stay safe."

    1. _____

    2. _____

    3. _____

3. Is the gain worth the price? Look at each sacrifice and
    each perceived gain. Ask yourself is it really worth it?

4. Choose to perceive each situation differently. Create a
    reality in your mind where no one loses in each situa-
    tion. If you have difficulty with this step, ask for
    guidance and allow yourself to be receptive for this
    guidance to come. Don't judge where it may come
    from—just be open.

    1. _____

    2. _____

    3. _____

3

No Blame = No Pain

*"A dying world asks only that you
rest an instant from attack on
yourself, that it be healed."* [1]

By now we realize that continuing the practice of sacrifice is both harmful and unnecessary. Understanding this is one thing, though; stopping it is another. We can understand conceptually that sacrifice is harmful, but changing old behavior patterns takes patience, practice and lots of diligence. Knowing that sacrifice is not only unnecessary but actually impossible does not mean that we won't be tempted to continue. We have held this practice and belief since the dawning of time, so it is important to be gentle with ourselves as we create new methods of behaving towards ourselves and one another.

As we learn the many ways in which we sacrifice, it is important to remember that it is much easier to replace an old, unhealthy, behavior pattern with a new, healthy one, than it is to simply attempt to stop the old pattern. It also helps to create phrases that remind us of our new behavior pattern. The old phrase "no pain = no gain" can be replaced with a new, more positive one: "**no blame = no pain.**" Blame, just like sacrifice always equals pain. We will inevitably find ourselves in a state of discomfort whenever we blame another or ourselves, for when we blame, we align ourselves with a state of victim consciousness: "you did this to me;" "if it weren't for you I wouldn't feel this way." The dynamics of blame are identical with the dynamics of sacrifice. When we blame another person, we are claiming our own innocence while judging another. We believe that someone must be guilty for another to be innocent.

To be innocent another must be guilty

I recently experienced this belief in a very powerful way. I was selected to perform the special music at a regional conference of ministers. This honored and excited me. I asked the person in charge what she needed from me for this occasion. She responded "Don't worry, I will handle everything. Just know that you are confirmed." I planned my schedule accordingly and made arrangements to sing and speak in nearby locations, since this conference was to be held in an area outside the U.S. where I had never been. I contacted the person in charge about three months prior to the conference. She had forgotten our conversation and had contracted with another musician to do the music. I was very disappointed. She was extremely apologetic, and she asked how she could make this up to me. Her suggestions included sending me money or helping me to do the music the following year. A few days after our conversation, I received a letter from her stating that she had met with the regional committee of ministers. They suggested that I was to blame for the misunderstanding because I had not received a contract, and I should have known that I had not been hired.

The purpose of this story is not to say that anyone was right or wrong. We all make mistakes. Rather, this story shows that no matter who we are, or what position we hold in society, we all have a tendency to assign blame. This group of ministers didn't want their fellow minister to feel guilty, and I agree. But they pointed the finger at me so she could let go of her guilt. I was to blame; I was responsible; I was guilty. This is the type of insanity we practice on a daily basis, and it is a perfect example of our guilt projection as discussed in Chapter One.

This reminds me of a conversation between Joseph Campbell and Bill Moyers in the TV series "The Power of Myth." They were discussing various metaphors concerning the creation of man, including the creation story from the Bible, which appears to have originated from an old African story. Both stories revolved around a man, a woman, a snake and some fruit, and in both stories God asked "why did you eat the fruit?" In both stories the man responded "the woman told me to," while the woman replied, "the snake told me to." Bill Moyers asked Joseph Campbell "where does the buck stop?" Well, the buck stops here with you and I, and it stops now if we choose, or else we will continue the "no pain=no gain" game.

Our entire legal system is based on blame, on the need to identify both an innocent party and a guilty party. We always seek the person who committed the wrong. Our laws are established to protect the innocent, but protect them from whom? We always assume there are those who must be guilty, but the truth is that we are all innocent, every single one of us. Until we understand this though, someone will be required to play the role of the guilty party.

Paul Ferrini in his book *Love Without Conditions* addresses this issue in a very bold manner. He suggests:

> *" Let us first take away your mask of moral superiority... Criminals are just one group of untouchables in your society. You do not want to look at their lives. You do not want to hear about their pain. You want*

to put them away where you do not
have to deal with them. You do the
same with the elderly, the mentally
ill, the homeless and so forth.

"You see, my friend, you do not
want the responsibility to love
your brother. Yet without loving
him, you cannot learn to love and
accept yourself. Your brother is the
key to your salvation. He always
was and always will be.

"Just as the individual denies and
represses the negative tendencies he
does not want to accept in himself,
society denies and institutionalizes
the problems it does not want to
face." [2]

We watch this drama unfold every day. A mother in South Carolina drowns her two children, and the community cries out for her death sentence. We see two "innocent" children die at the hands of their mother, and she becomes a monster. The community does not want to know her pain or her anguish, because it does not want to focus on its own. We are all wounded; acts such as this are driven by unacknowledged pain and guilt. If we acknowledge her pain, we also need to acknowledge our own—and there is a tremendous unwillingness to do this. We would rather focus our attention on another's actions, rather than understanding that those actions simply reflect our own fear and guilt. If we believe that we are incapable of such acts, or that we are different than this mother, we are only kidding ourselves. We heal when we extend love to this mother, for in loving her, we are forgiving ourselves.

It is far easier to blame those we perceive as being different: black, white, yellow, red, republicans and democrats, communists and capitalists, Serbs and Croatians, Christians and New Agers and so on. We are not as different from one another as we think, however, and the tide has begun to change. Recently we saw two arch-enemies, Yasser Arafat and Yitzhak Rabin, shaking hands and negotiating with President Clinton. Russia is choosing democracy and capitalism (let's suspend judgment on democracy and capitalism). The walls of separation are crumbling.

We also blame God

Have you ever blamed God for your circumstances? Every time we say that "God's will" for us is pain, we are blaming God for our miseries. Think about it. God didn't choose the pain or the blame. You did, to punish yourself, and you did it because that is how you were taught. Each time we believe that God brings us pain and misfortune, or that God's will for us is less-than-perfect happiness, we play the role of "victim of God" and thus continue to feel separate from God.

We stop blaming others for our conditions when we play the "No blame = No pain" game. We stop blaming God for our miseries and we stop blaming ourselves, which is *equally* important. We can greatly assist this healing process by practicing the game of "no blame = no pain" at work and at home. When you say "you did this to me" to someone, you are blaming that person. You are giving away your power and choosing to be separate from your fellow workers and family members. Remember, blaming someone *always* equals feeling separate. Why is this?

What is the purpose of blame?

What happens when we blame? We judge, and that judgment creates guilt, and that guilt creates the need for punishment. (Back to the need for sacrifice!) This is a vicious cycle, because if I feel deserving of punishment, I will choose pain, and then I will begin the cycle again. This reinforces the belief that the world is an unsafe place and that I must defend myself against it. What happens when I defend myself? I separate myself from you and from God by building walls of protection. We therefore perpetuate our pretense of being separate from God and each other.

I had a very wonderful experience of this recently. A group of my friends got together for dinner to plan an East Coast Miracles conference. After dinner the host shared his feelings about one of us who was moving from the area, and how he was experiencing abandonment and other related issues concerning this move. We progressed from those feelings to a healing of some of his major childhood issues. The experience affected us very deeply, and we moved into a very connected, unified, and holy space. After feeling this holy connection for a time, we talked about related issues in our own lives. I brought up a judgment I had made about my husband Patrick. This immediately broke the energy and we all felt the shift instantaneously. Through judging Patrick, I felt guilt and the need to punish myself. The energy in the room shifted from safe and holy to guarded. If I judged Patrick, why wouldn't I judge my friends as well?

Guilt is the sole cause of pain

Let us look again at the cycle of blame. When we blame, we judge; judgment creates guilt, and guilt creates the need for punishment. If I believe I deserve to be punished, I will begin the cycle again. Why? Because blame always leads to guilt, and guilt is the sole cause of pain. The cycle continues; I ask myself "How do I get rid of the guilt?" which also means "How do I get rid of the pain?" My initial response will be "I will attempt to give it away." I do that by blaming. This is exactly what Adam and Eve did in the creation story.

How do we stop? Do we throw away judgments? Do we condemn them? No! That judges the judgment and perpetuates the cycle of blame. Should we blame ourselves for blaming? No. We stop the pattern through acceptance: acceptance of ourselves exactly as we are, where we are, and who we are in this moment, acceptance of everything about ourselves and our lives. (We will discuss this process at length in Chapter 10). Paul Ferrini suggests:

> *" Be willing to look at the things you would condemn. That is the fastest way to dismantle your guilt."* [3]

As I mention elsewhere in this book, we must become aware of how we are playing the old game before we can leave it behind. This comprises a large part of the acceptance process—examining how we make others wrong. Do we accuse others of being responsible for our own unhappiness? Do we accuse others of being the cause of our pain? **Any time** you feel pain, look to see if you are blaming someone (remember, this includes yourself). Again, the cycle that precedes pain is: I blame, I feel guilt, and I feel the need to be punished.

I still blame my husband. Imagine blaming someone and getting upset because they choose to do a chore differently from you. I know it is ludicrous, but I still find myself doing it. We have different ways of doing chores; we have different styles around the house. Patrick is a pretty casual guy. For him, stuff is just stuff, but I feel that we should take care of our possessions. I have clothes in my closet that are 10 years old and look brand new and some are a lot older than that. These are clothes that I wear year in and year out. Pat, on the other hand, goes through a shirt or a new pair of pants in a matter of months, sometimes even weeks. It is the same with furniture. I blame him when there is a scratch in our new glass coffee table, because he puts his feet on it. That may seem reasonable to many of us, but it causes pain: pain because I am protecting my coffee table; pain because I have chosen to be angry and view the table as being more important than my husband's comfort; pain because I need to feel right; and, perhaps pain to him because I become a nag.

We can stop this pattern by accepting that we are still playing the blame game, acknowledging how we are continuing it, and thus discontinuing the pattern, and, ultimately, looking at the situation differently. I understand that we all have our own ways of doing things, our own styles. None of these are "right" or "wrong." It is much easier for me to release my judgments than to continue to be upset by my partner's idiosyncrasies, (unless I still want to be right). A silly example: I see some towels as kitchen hand towels, others as dish towels, various size bathroom towels, old towels that can be used as rag towels, and so on. Pat sees them all as the same, however, so he will grab any towel to do whatever chore is at hand—cleaning up grease, wiping the floor, cleaning up spilled paint. I asked him to use only rags for these occasions. I didn't get the response I wished for, and after a while I decided that there were no "sacred towels." All towels are equal; and when we need new ones, I go to the store.

The old games don't work anymore

I have discovered that my old ways of reacting to people no longer work for me, as the following story will illustrate. In June of 1993, I contracted to do my weekend gig at a church in San Jose, CA. The minister, Rev. Carole, and I hit it off over the phone like we were long lost friends, and we very much looked forward to my visit the following February. I sent a follow up letter that discussed matters such as my financial needs. I didn't hear back and assumed that my terms were acceptable. The following January, I called to discuss final details and was surprised to hear that the financial arrangements were not acceptable, my letter had been lost, and that they could not possibly give me what I had requested. In fact, I would receive no payment for the morning services since their minister was to attend. My reaction was less than favorable: as you can guess, it was to blame. I first thought: "well, this is a fine time to tell me, one month before the job. I can't fill in with another gig; you should have been responsible and told me this months ago. After all, I am on tour and I have expenses like airfare, and I don't like working for nothing."

Unfortunately, I talked with the minister within minutes of hearing the news, while I was still engaged in playing the blame game, with myself in the victim role. I attempted to be nice on the surface while I talked to Carole, but underneath I wanted to make her wrong. As you can imagine, it was a very unsatisfactory conversation. I was blaming her and she was understandably defending herself, since I was in attack mode. The job was still up in the air when we got off the phone, but I felt terrible. I felt physically sick, emotionally violated, and just plain awful. **And**, I knew that my feelings had **nothing** to do with Carole or the job. I intended to make her wrong, but in so doing I really attacked myself. In times past, I could blame and believe that I felt really good. "How dare they do this to me? How unprofessional they are! Why don't they get their act together?" Of course, I was really talking about myself. I felt unprofessional. I didn't feel that my act was together, and therefore this happened to me. I was unwilling to look at the truth though, and instead projected my unworthy feelings onto others.

It was very clear to me after this conversation that I can no longer make anyone wrong, including myself. It doesn't work and only makes me feel sick. Believe it or not, this is real progress, for I no longer need to play the right/wrong game. I can truly live in the knowledge that all things do work together for good, without exception. And I know that trying to make another person wrong not only does not work, it has very painful consequences. Blame *does* equal pain, physical, emotional, and immediate pain. Once you begin to live in the state of peace, love and joy, leaving that state becomes increasingly painful, and you avoid anything that could cause that to happen.

Carole called a few days later. I apologized for attempting to make her wrong, and we had a wonderful conversation. I shared with her the many gifts that came from the prior conversation. I didn't care if she apologized for the mix up, since I knew in my heart that I had "hired" Carole to play this role. I understood that the old games just don't work anymore. My weekend at this church was absolutely wonderful. The Sunday services went very well, the playshop was full, and I stayed longer and gave more counseling sessions than I had ever done while on tour. I stayed with Carole that weekend and it was as if we had been long-lost friends coming together once again. She asked me to return when she takes some time off. My acknowledging the truth about my part of the game freed me to do the work that I love; I stepped out of the victim role and received the abundance of the Universe.

Remember, these patterns of blame are ingrained in our brains. We create a groove in our brain with each new habit, which is why it becomes a habit. We need to create a new and deeper groove to stop blaming, a new pattern of thinking and behaving that supports rather than belittles, inspires rather than criticizes. The less we blame, the less pain we will feel, and the more we will feel the love that we all are. We can begin to claim responsibility for our lives. And, we can claim our power by **not** pointing the finger at our neighbor or ourselves. It is a new way of living. It's time to leave a new legacy to our children. It's time to practice a new way of behaving and a new way of thinking.

When we stop blaming, we will no longer need an innocent party and a guilty party. When we stop blaming ourselves and others for our predicaments, we will stop playing out the victim's role. When we stop blaming, we will no longer feel guilty. Perhaps most importantly, when we stop blaming, we will stop choosing to believe in our separation from one another and from God, because blaming **always** equals *feeling* separate.

So let's all practice together. Let's play the No Blame = No Pain game.

Exercises

1. Do you feel that you or another is responsible for your happiness and well-being?

2. Do you believe that the misfortunes in your life or any lack or limitations are God's will?

3. Where do you choose to play the victim? Example: "You make me feel_____." "You won't let me_____."

   1. _____

   2. _____

   3. _____

4. Choose to see all parties as innocent. Choose to see the love of God in each participant.

4

Thanksliving

A STORY:

> *God was talking with St. Peter in heaven one day and said: "So many people are praying for so many things: all the saints and angels are so busy. There is one person on earth who keeps repeating the prayer 'thank you God, thank you.' Give him anything he wants."*

An old saying goes "Give thanks for all things, for all things come from God." I believe the first half of this statement to be very helpful, but the second half states that all *things* come from God. This means that God sends not only the things that we like, but also the difficulties, the sorrows, and the pain. No "thing" comes from God; all things are brought to us by our own creative power and our level of conscious awareness. What we *believe* to be true becomes our reality, our environment. We attract what we believe we can have, or feel that we deserve. We determine whether a thing, circumstance, or event is good or bad, and we do that by our programming and the various beliefs that we hold. Look at your environment—your relationships, job, home, financial situation, health. What you see there is what you want, or feel that you deserve. To put it another way, you have what you want. I know that some of you are thinking "But I don't *want* what I *have*." Let me explain.

What you have or don't have reflects your beliefs. This holds true in all areas of our lives. If you believe relationships are hard, guess what? Either yours will seem hard, or you won't be in one at all. If you don't trust yourself or others, untrustworthy people will show up in your life. Our mind continuously exposes itself, and therefore your environment can reflect only what your mind believes. Why then is it helpful to give thanks for all things, especially when some of those things are events we don't like, or are circumstances we judge as bad, or identify our limiting beliefs?

Give thanks for ALL things

The theme of "Thanksliving" was suggested many years ago while I did inner listening. I was told "Give thanks for all things." I asked, "all things?" I was told "YES, ALL THINGS!" It was suggested to me that I look at my life as it was and give thanks for **all** of it.

Let's do that right now. Take a moment and close your eyes. Look at and be present with your life as it is right now. Examine what is on your plate currently—your present friends, relationships, family, job situation, home situation, political situation, current spiritual understanding—and say "**Thank You**" for everything that is in your life right now.

I heard that! Someone just asked "Do I have to mean it? Must it be sincere?" Be as sincere as you can, to the very best of your ability at this moment. If you really have difficulty, just say "thank you" anyway, and add a thank-you for the difficulty in feeling thankful.

At the time in my life when this happened (many years ago, remember) there were certain aspects of my life that I did not like. I asked my inner voice if that meant that I also should thank the I.R.S. for the field audit we were going through? "YES." Every time I get sick I am to say thank you for the illness? "YES." I should say thank you to the person who murdered my brother? "YES." I should say "thank you" for the good *and* the bad? Guess what the answer was— "YES!" I was told to put my trust in God and not in my own understanding, for all things work together for good.

Today I no longer believe that there is good vs. bad. There is only God, which I believe is all-loving. There is nothing "bad" in the Universe. Our perception of events around us causes us to experience peace or pain. We all have experienced events that, upon reflection, we know to have been purposeful, although we didn't have the perspective to see the whole picture at the time. When we're in the forest, often all we see is the tree in front of us.

I have learned over the years that I have two choices in any situation: I can be grateful, or I can be angry. Which choice do you suppose provides more peace and acceptance? Gratitude, clearly. You may not understand or like a situation, but saying "thank you" allows us to return to a state of peace with little struggle or effort. This was not clear to me thirteen years ago, so my inner voice suggested that I do the following exercises.

1. Every experience has molded us into who we are now

I was told to reflect on my life, understanding that everything I have experienced has molded me into the person I am now, with a deeper understanding and realization of who I truly am. My career changes provided skills that I now use on a daily basis. My previous marriages taught me what does and does not work in relationships. My brother's death taught me that in fact there is no "death," since he came back and talked to my mother, my husband, and me on several occasions. We not only heard him but felt his physical presence. The audit taught me that I.R.S. workers are also children of God, and I no longer fear the I.R.S. (Since that audit, which was the third in a row, I have not been audited again.)

A friend of mine recently came to the same understanding. The State of Virginia informed Doug that they would be looking at his records for the preceding two years. They amended that request, first saying that they wanted the last three years, and then the last seven years. Doug found being grateful for all of this a little difficult. When the auditor arrived, however, an overwhelming rush of energy came over Doug that said "This man is your savior. He is your Brother. Be grateful." So Doug became very grateful for this auditor. The agent told Doug: "This is the neatest set of books I have ever seen." He was so impressed by their neatness, and Doug's acceptance of his presence, that he simply leafed through Doug's records, without paying attention to the numbers.

As the audit progressed, a level of trust grew between them, and they worked together in harmony. Doug chose gratitude, to see this man as his savior, and chose not to react from fear. The outcome was better than he had hoped. The agent said that he would be sending Doug a very small bill, around $300, and he parted in wonderful spirits, thanking Doug for such a great experience!

2. All problems bring gifts within them

Seeing problems as gifts or opportunities puts you in the driver's seat. When we say "thank you" for everything in our lives, we look at everything in our lives from a positive point of view, thereby turning the "problems" in our lives into opportunities. As my favorite quote in Richard Bach's book *Illusions* says: *"There is no such thing as a problem without a gift for you in its hands. You seek problems because you need their gifts."*[1]

We usually play the victim when we are not grateful. I would venture to guess that we all know what it feels like to play this role. As victims, we feel powerless and fear-filled, and we become defensive because we feel the need to protect ourselves. And, *A Course in Miracles* states: *"If I defend myself I am attacked."*[2] When we are grateful, therefore, we do not feel the need to attack.

3. What we focus on expands

Whatever we put our attention on expands in our awareness. Put your attention on pain and it grows. Likewise, being thankful will attract into your life much for which to be thankful.

The following story will illustrate this point. A single mother with several children purchased a house that she really did not like. She felt it was all she could afford, however. After moving, she decided that she really hated the house, but she also believed that she did not have money to fix it up. She was miserable, and focused on all the aspects of the house she didn't like: the house needed a new kitchen, every room needed painting, every window needed drapes.

After months of feeling sorry for herself, she read an article on gratitude that suggested that she give thanks for those things that she could be grateful for, rather than focusing on those she could not. She started by being grateful for the roof over their heads. She gave thanks for the stove and refrigerator, the beds for each child, and for the money to pay the mortgage. She thanked the house for protecting her from the elements. Within days of pretending to be grateful, she felt the gratitude become real. Soon she had enough money to purchase some paint, and someone gave her wallpaper. Little by little, the house became her dream house. It took time and creativity, but the result was a home that she loved and in which she took pride. She attributed this transformation to her giving thanks, though at times it was difficult.

Start giving thanks on a daily basis for those people, circumstances and events in our lives for which we are genuinely grateful. We then can easily give thanks when we experience challenges because it has become a daily habit.

4. Gratitude increases our physical well being

On a physical level, being thankful opens our bodies to good health. Our cells expand and open when we are thankful. An attitude of gratitude is synonymous with an attitude of acceptance. When someone gives us a gift, we say "Thank you, I will accept it." It is easy to be grateful when someone is about to give us something that we want. But what happens to our bodies when we receive something that we don't think we want? We get tense and our cells shut down. We say "No! I don't want that," and our bodies say "No!" to life.

When we express gratitude we are rejoicing, and this message is sent to each and every cell in the body. "Rejoice" means "to feel joy," and our bodies align in harmony with the Universe when we feel joy. We feel alive and healthy. When we are angry, resentful, and bitter—when we don't live from an attitude of gratitude—we contract, as do the cells in our bodies. We close down and we stop the flow of harmony. This eventually causes disease and the death of our bodies.

If we do experience a health challenge, we should give thanks for whatever the challenge may be. I know many, many people who have expressed thanks for life-threatening situations, regardless of the outcome. Several of my friends have died of AIDS and every one was grateful for the experience and its many gifts. Several other friends have had miraculous reversals of diseases such as cancer and AIDS, and all are equally grateful for the experiences. Each has said that the gifts far outweigh the discomfort or pain. Lou Gehrig on "Lou Gehrig Day" at Yankee Stadium said: "You've been reading about my bad break for weeks now. But today I think I'm the luckiest man alive. I now feel more than ever that I have much to live for."

5. Gratitude breaks the "blame cycle"

Gratitude breaks the cycle of judgment, guilt, and pain, which we discussed in the previous chapter, because gratitude leads us into the state of acceptance. Being grateful for all things really means that I accept all things. Gratitude is another name for forgiveness.

A couple of years ago I officiated at a wedding of two very charming people. The warm and beautiful ceremony was followed by a delightful party in their Berkeley Hills home. I saw the husband two months later. He shared that, within the last three months, his best friend had died of cancer, his wife had left him within days after their honeymoon, and he had lost his home and his possessions in the Berkeley Hills fire. The only things he had left were the clothes on his back and his car (which died the following week). He spoke of having an attitude of gratitude, and said that he was indeed grateful. At the same time, he expressed his pain and he asked me to accompany him to the site of his house and perform a ceremony to release the past.

As we drove up into the Berkeley Hills, I felt as though we had been suddenly transported to the Moon's surface. For blocks there was nothing but ash, charcoal, a few dead trees, and the remains of water heaters that were bent into weird, twisted shapes. He asked me what I thought of the scene, I had no words; it was simply indescribable. As we got to where his house had been located, he walked up to a dead oak tree and said good-bye. Crying, he said: "This might

sound very strange to you, but I feel a deep sense of gratitude. I don't understand it. I have nothing. And yet, I feel
this amazingly deep sense of gratitude to God. I know that
God is giving me this sense of gratitude. I know that I of
myself could not feel this, but somehow God is allowing me
to feel grateful for all of this. I feel pain. I feel anger. I feel
sorrow. But, at the same time, I feel all this gratitude. I know
I could go out and get an architect and draw up plans for a
new house. And I could look for a new girlfriend, but six
months from now I'd probably find some reason to kill her
and wonder where all the rage was coming from. Right now,
I just need to feel my feelings and feel gratitude for my life
just the way it is. I need to accept all of this, not deny it; **be
grateful,** and then I can move on." What a teacher!

I stood there and thought "I'm not sure that I could do
this. I am not sure that if I lost everything I would be this
grateful." What I did know, however, was that he was primed
to receive the support that God was giving to him in that
moment because he so willingly gave his life to God every
single day. Every single day he affirms that he is powerless
without God, that he believes that God restores him to a state
of bliss, sanity and grace. He gives his life every day to that
God, and that God, that Higher Power, gave him the grace
to be able to feel gratitude during this time in his life. The
next time I saw him, he was renting a wonderful home in
Contra Costa County, and all his needs were being met. He
felt grateful through all of this. He wasn't sure why, but it
was there.

I know that I am always exactly where I am supposed to
be. My basic teaching is that we (you and I) are the love of
God. Being grateful allows us to remember this teaching. It
permits us to remember that all things work together for
good, even though we may not know what that "good" is
when we are in the middle of a pain-filled experience. Practicing gratitude on a daily basis makes it easier to be grateful
in those times when we don't see a reason to be grateful.

A Course in Miracles states that:

> **" Problems are not specific, but they
> take specific forms, and these
> specific shapes make up the world.
> And no one understands the nature
> of his problem."** [3]

Einstein said that a problem cannot be solved at the level at which it was created. Being grateful lifts us above the level of the problem and realigns us with truth. It provides a new perspective and helps us to find answers that elude us at the level of chaos. Years ago, I was given a metaphor during meditation to explain this concept. In the meditation was a big, black pot. I could hear the words "toil, boil, trouble and bubble," which reminded me of the witches' pot in Shakespeare's *MacBeth*. I was guided to look into the pot, and I saw problems that people were experiencing. I then was guided to jump into the pot. Reluctantly I did and felt as though I was being swallowed by the problems. There was no perspective, no distance, no ability to do anything except focus my attention on the problems. I felt as though I had been absorbed. Soon I was released from the pot and I understood that we are only absorbed further into a problem when we try to solve it at its own level. Only by stepping back from the pot (the problem) can we gain perspective. Gratitude allows us to step back.

We will remember that we are the love of God when we practice gratitude. We will attract only that for which it will be easy to be grateful. When we forget the truth, when we focus on ideas or situations that appear to be less than perfect, we need to practice an attitude of gratitude for *all* things.

Remember, it is only our perception—how we see and interpret situations—that make them good or bad, happy or sad.

6. Gratitude changes the way we think

Let me say that again, as it bears repeating: *gratitude changes the way we think.* Gratitude allows us to change the pattern of belief that we are guilty, and thus separate, and thus deserving of pain, for gratitude changes our perception of ourselves.

Because gratitude creates acceptance, we no longer need to reject our fears. This is very important, because rejecting fear only creates more fear, more separation, and more guilt and pain. Being grateful brings us into a state of forgiveness and love. Love and fear cannot co-exist. Saying "thank you" changes the way we react to one another and to seemingly negative situations. It changes our belief that we deserve punishment and pain. Gratitude allows us to accept ourselves, and to accept ourselves is to love ourselves.

It is very easy to be grateful for everyone and everything in our lives, because they reveal our beliefs to us. Every time someone comes up and "pushes one of your buttons," every time you experience fear, you are acknowledging a belief that you have about your world. For this we can be truly thankful, because once the belief is uncovered it can be discarded. I hear a phrase over and over again in 12-step meetings: "Uncover, discover and discard." Gratitude is a way of saying "Rejoice! I am letting go of another block to love's awareness. "

In our ACIM group the other evening, a man shared that "If I think a part of me is bad or wrong (my ego self), I am going to make that part of me stronger by setting up defenses against it. If I treat it as a fearful little child who is in fact safe, then I accept myself."

He said that he had realized this after an incident that had occurred earlier that day at school. He is a kindergarten

teacher, and one of his pupils was behaving in a very destructive way. He went over to the child, held him, and said:
"It's okay, I understand, you are safe. You are safe." The child
calmed down immediately and allowed his teacher to hold
him. The child accepted that he was in a safe environment,
and no longer felt the need to misbehave.

Gratitude = acceptance = love. Practice saying "thank you"
for every feeling, every situation, and every circumstance.
Remember, gratitude changes the way you think. Mind creates reality, and thus changing our mind changes our reality.

Gratitude = acceptance = love = the world becomes a safe
place = the end of the illusion = the end of separation.

Exercises

1. Make a gratitude list. Write down all the people,
   circumstances, and things for which you are grateful.

2. On a daily basis, start to give thanks for people, circumstances, and things in your life.

3. Examine several areas of your life where you find it
   difficult to feel gratitude, and identify at least one thing
   for which you are in fact grateful. (If you do not like
   your job, for example, give thanks that you have a job,
   and give thanks for the paycheck that you do get. If
   you do not like where you live give thanks that you
   have somewhere to live.)

Do the following three exercises at one sitting.
4. List at least three things (people or situations) for
   which you are grateful.

5. List three areas in your life where you find it difficult
   to be grateful and the reason why: "I am not grateful

for _____because
_____.

6. Reframe the statements from number 5 by finding at least one gift in each for which you can be grateful. You might choose to write: "I am grateful to _____ for _____ because I've learned _____or I've changed _____.

An example for #5:
5. I am not grateful for my husband or wife because I feel like he (she) is always making me wrong.

An example for #6:
6. I am grateful for my husband or wife because I've learned that other peoples' opinions of me are just that: their opinion. It does not mean that I am wrong or bad or inferior. I can be free of the opinions of those around me.

5

Victim, Victor, Vehicle: Stages Along the Spiritual Path

> *" I think that when we're in heaven*
> *we'll be having such a wonderful*
> *time looking at God that we will*
> *not want to have an individual*
> *experience"* [1]
>
> —Joseph Campbell

Rev. Carol Ruth Knox, former minister of Unity of Walnut Creek, once gave a great talk entitled "Victim, Victor, Vehicle" that explained the transformation we experience on our journey toward awakening. She described three stages of awareness: "victim," "victor," and "vehicle." As "victims" we perceive all around us to be responsible for all of our circumstances: our pain, our loneliness, our poverty, our happiness, our well being.

As "victors" we become aware that we are the masters of our own destiny and the creators of our own environment. We flex our creative muscles through the practice of "demonstrations." One usually starts small creating parking places when and where you want them, for example. Then one advances to more difficult or challenging manifestations such as attracting the perfect mate or finding the exact make and model car you want. Once one understands that the world is ours to command, one attempts to master the "victor" role.

Finally, we become "vehicles," surrendering to God's will and saying, "Thy will be done." This stage is definitely the most fun, and by far the safest. By attempting to create what I *thought* I wanted, I often chose things that often brought me exciting challenges, rather than the happiness I expected. As *A Course in Miracles* puts it:

> *" You must have noticed an outstanding characteristic of every end that the ego has accepted as its own. When you have achieved it, it has not satisfied you."*[2]

I had a very vivid dream while writing this chapter. I was in a vehicle that looked like a trolley car. It was effortlessly going up and down the streets of San Francisco, always staying right on track. I suddenly realized that I could not see anyone at the wheel, so I jumped up from my relaxed, peaceful posture and grabbed the wheel. As soon as I did, it became very difficult to keep the car in its lane. I suddenly found myself at the wheel of a very crowded trolley car at the crest of an extremely steep hill. I became very frightened, wondering if the brakes would work. I felt I could not control the car, and I looked for an escape.

Surrender

This dream was very clear to me. When I try to live my life on MY terms, I become overwhelmed and fearful. I don't know what to do, and I want to escape. When I give my life daily to God, making my decisions together with my Higher Power, I can enjoy the ride and not worry about my destination. I trust that I will arrive safely, and that the journey will be fun.

I was taught that one cannot skip steps in the Spiritual awakening process. But isn't that the old belief that life is a classroom, in which we must pass a series of tests in order to be worthy of our natural state of bliss? Perhaps the victor state is necessary for some, but it revolves around control and manipulation. It seems to me that this stage is just another ego choice.

The sooner we are willing to turn our will and our lives over to the care of God, the sooner our lives will become manageable. *A Course in Miracles* states that:

> *" You cannot make decisions by yourself. The only question really is with what you choose to make them."*[3]

You have two choices: your limited ego self or your unlimited God Self. Is there really a choice? Actually, yes. We can listen to the self that sabotages us, or the Self that supports us. And until we become extremely vigilant in our thoughts, we will at times continue to align with ego, thinking: "I want it MY way!"

Why not skip steps, jumping right into God's will? Surely God sees more of the picture than I. Surely my Holy Self believes in my worthiness more than I. I can trust that God's choice for me will be based in love and abundance. An example of this occurred quite recently for my husband and me. Since we were moving to an area in which snow abounds, we thought it would be a good idea to get a 4-wheel-drive vehicle. Neither of us were comfortable in the big van-type vehicles, and we wanted a nice car that we could use for all occasions. I sold my 1983 Honda Prelude and looked for our new car, without success. I asked my Holy Self for the perfect vehicle. (I figured my Holy Self knew where we were going and what we liked and needed better than us.) Within two days, we saw an ad for a Suburu SVX, with which we were unfamiliar. We had test-driven a Suburu Legacy, but it did not have the power we wanted for driving around our new home at an elevation of 6000 feet. We went to see this and bought it that day! It was *more* than we had hoped for: a luxury, high performance all-wheel-drive vehicle. We also paid only a little more than we would have for a new Legacy, because Suburu was giving substantial dealer incentives to sell the SVX.

The process was effortless and extremely rewarding. Instead of solving the problem by myself (a path aligned with my ego: "Mother I'd rather do it myself"), I aligned with my true Self, and the outcome was more than I could have imagined. The sooner we surrender to the idea that God's will for us is joy, happiness, abundance and peace, the sooner we surrender to God's will. Why not now? Why continue in the old pattern, which didn't work well anyway?

Looking at this through the metaphor in Chapter One, we have played in the first two stages since we incarnated. The child in the metaphor believed she was the victim of her parents (Mother/Father God). She chose to be the victor by running away from home, thus creating and ruling her own world (as we do with the world each of us perceives). By creating **this** world the way **we think we want** it, we make the original mistake again and again.

Surrender to God's will is the safest and quickest way home to peace and joy. This will result in our perfect happiness, and isn't that worth the price of surrender?

Many people ask me "this surrender concept sounds like a wonderful idea, but how do I do it?" Actually, it's easy— you simply make the decision to surrender. You may have to choose several times before it becomes a habit. It's impossible to *plan* how to surrender; it is a process. You conclude that there is a better way than trying to do it all by yourself, and inevitably you give up trying. You then have chosen to align your decision-making with the power of the Universe.

"But how do I know who is choosing, the self or the Self?" That takes practice. Some of us hear a quiet, peaceful voice, some get gut feelings, and some simply *know*. But each of us will hear if we learn to listen. The answer may come in many different forms: an ad in a newspaper for a Suburu, a friend who calls you to talk, a minister's sermon, a comic strip. One of the most consistent sources for answers is in meditation. The most important thing to remember is the intent—simply choose to align with your Self, and know that it is done. Don't try and make a big deal out of it, or analyze, or second guess. Remember, your "self" is nothing more than what you believe about yourself anyway, so choosing what is right for your highest and best good will naturally mean making the "right" choice.

Undoing

Most of us go through several stages on the journey to enlightenment. Webster's dictionary defines "enlightened" as "freedom from ignorance and misinformation." Our journey therefore is as much a process of undoing old behavior patterns, old belief systems, and old ideas as it is anything else. I have suggested that we can skip steps, and indeed we can, but it takes a lot of willingness on our part, and requires a total commitment to patience, humor, and, above all, the acceptance of ourselves *wherever* we are in the process.

Perhaps the most difficult concept to embrace is the realization that we create our own world. We attract all that happens to us. This may be a hard pill to swallow, because we are accustomed to believing that we bear no responsibility for that which happens to us. We are familiar and comfortable with the role of victim. It is easier to accept that the painful events that have occurred in our lives were the doing of someone else than it is to acknowledge our own responsibility.

A friend of mine recently shared a wonderful story about her relationship with her boss. Bea was the manager of a real estate company. She is a very hard and conscientious worker and took her role as manager very seriously. She felt that her boss had her under a microscope, judging her every action, and she believed that she was not meeting her boss's expectations. Bea felt more and more uncomfortable at work and became extremely stressed, both physically and emotionally. She also began to be afraid to make decisions because they might not meet her boss's approval.

One day she screwed up her courage, walked into her boss's office, and shared her feelings. Her boss was amazed. She had no idea that Bea felt this way, and in fact had been extremely pleased with Bea's performance. Bea had made herself into a victim of her boss, putting her boss in the role of judge, and all the while her boss was oblivious of this. Bea realized that she had projected her own judgments of herself onto her boss, and they now have a wonderful relationship.

One pitfall of this process occurs when we accept responsibility for everything that has occurred in our lives, because we focus on all the painful experiences we drew to ourselves. If you have a life-threatening disease, or you have a family to support and you lose your job, you may not want to accept your responsibility for attracting this into your life. Many years ago I watched a talk show with a panel of guests that included Terry Cole Whitaker. The panel was asked: "Do we in fact create our own realities? Do we attract to us all that happens to us?" Terry Cole Whitaker suggested that she could choose what she believes about this. She could believe that she did not create her reality, making her a victim and therefore powerless to do anything about her circumstances.

Or, she could accept responsibility for attracting her circumstances, enabling her to change them. She asked the TV host: "Which position would you rather be in?"

Remember to look for the gift

Initially, you might be tempted to experience guilt, wondering why you did this to yourself? We can move beyond this if we remember that there is a gift in every situation, no matter what the situation looks or feels like. In *The Courage to Change* a book for members of Al-Anon, a member expresses her gratitude for the gift of Alcoholism in her family:

> *" For me, alcoholism has proven to be a bittersweet legacy—bitter because of the pain I suffered, and sweet, because if it weren't for that pain, I wouldn't have searched for and found a better way of living."* [4]

There is a reason why we create events in our lives. We all have blocks to the awareness of love's presence, and we need to identify these blocks in order to remove them. To do this, we bring people and events into our lives to assist us in removing these blocks. Sometimes we need only a gentle reminder, while at other times the universe will provide us with the proverbial two-by-four when gentle reminders did not get our attention.

My husband ignored a gentle reminder in the form of a minor accident with our new Suburu. This happened during a time of great tension between us, but instead of asking for the gift that the Universe provided he focused on our tension. Two days later, he fell from our roof while painting our new house, severely injuring his leg. He was in surgery for five-and-a-half hours, and stayed on crutches for over four months. He ignored the gentle reminder, and the Universe provided a major two-by-four (perhaps this was an eight-by-ten)! This time he listened, and the resultant gifts have been many, especially with our relationship.

It becomes much easier to respond to the various challenges we experience when we understand that the universe is totally neutral, and that we provide its only meaning. In addition, we will understand that all events support us when we remember that the Universe is our support system, as long as we are willing to listen to the message.

Honor where you are

Those of us in the helping professions often hear and say "I should know better," "I should be further along in my process by now," and "Why can't I get it right?"

This is **NOT** helpful! All of us do the best we can or the best way we know. Much, if not all, of what we do is based on past programming, as though we live in the past rather than the present. We base our decisions on information we currently have, which comes from our past experience and knowledge. We therefore access our memory banks to choose how to act in our daily activities. If you observe yourself during a day, you will find yourself relying on past experience for present choices, such as stopping at a red light and choosing items from a menu. You also rely on past experiences when you react with disgust or delight to various people you contact during the day.

One day, you decide to change. You will react differently. You will send love to that fellow employee who's been getting under your skin for the last five years. You are going to be kind and understanding to your ex, with whom you have been angry since your divorce. All goes well, and then he/

she does something you really don't like. *Viola!* You think or
say something nasty.

What is the very next thing you do? If you truly have decided to behave differently, you'll probably turn on yourself, thinking "Well I flunked that," or "Why can't I be more
loving?" or "When am I going to learn?" Beating ourselves
up is just as harmful and useless as wanting to beat someone
else up, and it seems to be something we all do. But it does
not help, serving only to keep alive our limited belief about
ourselves.

We become the victim of ourselves

We used to point the finger at those outside ourselves. When
we accept that we are not victims of anyone else, we suddenly see that the hand pointing the finger has three fingers
pointing back at us. This is the next stage of the process.
Unfortunately, what usually occurs next is that we blame
ourselves instead of blaming others. Understanding our responsibility for what we attract in our lives, and our subse-
quent reactions, has nothing to do with blame, but we blame
so often that we automatically turn that blame on ourselves.
Again, this is not helpful! As we discussed in Chapter Three,
blame only produces pain. And when we think this way, we
become our own victim. In fact, we still play the victim. If
Patrick had focused blame on himself after he fell off the roof,
he would not have realized the many gifts available to him.
He probably would not have healed as quickly as he did
(which was miraculous to the doctor), and he may very well
have received yet another two-by-four from the Universe.

Let's face it—we all have Ph.D.'s in dysfunctional behavior. We've all learned from parents, teachers, and a variety of
role models how to do things the painful way. Until recently,
we've all been students in a school that teaches how it does
not work. Instead, we should think of ourselves as toddlers

in nursery school, learning how to think, choose, act, and behave all over again. Instead of being hard on ourselves, we should relax and enjoy learning to be kind and loving persons for ourselves and others.

Look at it this way. Wilt Chamberlain and Magic Johnson were considered to have been tops in the basketball world. If you asked either Wilt or Magic to pick up a violin and play it, would you expect them to play the violin with the same skill as they played basketball? Of course not. But that is what you expect of yourself. You are not an expert at changing your focus after two weeks or two years. Remember, you have the equivalent of a doctorate in how to behave in a painful way. That took time, and it's going to take time to learn new ways of behaving. Think of yourself as a toddler just beginning to walk. How would you treat this little child? Would you encourage her and cheer her on as she took her first steps, or would you reprimand the child because she fell down after walking for the first time? Encourage and praise yourself in the same way when you take the first, second, and third steps. When you forget and fall down, don't criticize or insult yourself. Tell yourself it is okay, and try again. Above all...

Be gentle with yourself

This is a concept that few of us were taught as children, and thus most haven't practiced this idea much. It does help a lot, however. Honoring ourselves wherever we are in our process is very beneficial and loving.

Remember, you are changing at least one lifetime of habitual responses, so be patient with yourself. When you find yourself being impatient, forgive yourself and work on the exercises at the end of this chapter. We have not decided with our Higher Power when we punish ourselves. Instead, we have aligned with our limited self and judgment.

Again, we can make all our decisions with God, including the thoughts we think—we choose the thoughts we have. That is a revealing exercise. Watch yourself for ten minutes or an hour if you can, choosing your thoughts. Please, be amused! Laugh at yourself when you fall short of your perceived goals of extending love, forgiveness, and releasing judgment. Lighten up! Many of us take enlightenment as very serious business, but the word speaks for itself: enlightenment = to illuminate = to be filled with light. So, lighten up and be gentle with yourself. Don't take the process or your place in it too seriously. It is much easier to change our patterns when we are amused, rather than horrified, at our behaviors.

We often choose our old behavior patterns because they work so well. We have become masters at sabotage. As I said earlier, we all have Ph.D.'s in dysfunctional behavior. It takes diligence and compassion with ourselves and each other to change.

Because it works

(I mentioned in the preface that this book would include several forms. The following section is guidance that I received during inner listening concerning behavior patterns.)

Question: "Why do I repeat the same patterns over and over which always result in emotional pain?"

Answer: *"First, let me assure you that emotional pain is no different than any other form of perceived pain. Pain is always a choice, and is always a choice to feel separated. Why do you choose the same patterns over and over again, ones that cause you to feel separate and therefore in pain? Because you know the pattern works. It achieves its purpose. This may sound oversimplified, but it is not. As you have discovered, there are only two perceived states of* *mind, love or pain (and pain is always fear). The only Real state of mind is love. When you are in pain therefore, you believe in something that is not real. You try to make it complicated, you think of yourself as complicated, but you are not. You are simply love.*

"You repeat the pattern (you often call it a "lesson") over and over again because you feel that it has worked before, and that it will work again. You feel peace for minutes, or hours, or days, but then decide you cannot continue to have this much peace. Instead you focus on the lack of peace by creating chaos through your own actions or your perception of someone else's actions.

"Let us look at an example. You have decided that being on time is important. So you become anxious when you find yourself running late. (Remember, the anxiety results from your choice for fear). When you are alone, you usually allow yourself plenty of time. When you are with someone else, however, you do not control that person. You decide that there is not enough time, and that the other person will not be ready. You feel this in your body. You become anxious, which you feel as pain. Whether or not you arrive at your desired destination on time is not the issue. You feel the pain, even if you do arrive on time (which you almost always do). This pattern is fail-safe. Your ego self knows it works and uses it over and over and over.

"Understand what you are doing. See the pattern. Watch yourself choose it. Recognize how you sabotage your peace, and in that moment choose again. Initially choosing to repeat the pattern does not mean you need to play it out to the end. What is the end anyway? Who chooses to stop this repetitive game, and at what point during the process? You do. You can choose at any moment to stop the pattern and choose peace instead."

Post Script 8-31-93

As I have suggested in other parts of this book, the Universe is a perfect support system; all is always in Divine order. This has been pointed out to me over and over no matter how hard I have tried to sabotage my life.

I really have resisted writing this book. The Universe recently has opened space for me to write it. I therefore committed yesterday to complete this book by the end of 1994, and I received guidance to begin work each and every morning at 8 AM. I am sure you know what I am going to say next. Many things came up this morning that took more time than normal, and I started feeling anxious about starting on time. When I finally sat down at the computer, I found my notes on the above guidance. The synchronicity of finding this guidance on this morning was highly supportive. I did not remember the example that was used while writing the guidance last winter, but I did remember how struck I was with the concept's simplicity. The most wonderful feeling of peace came over me as I read it. I am being supported. Commitment does work, and we are not alone in anything. We are always guided, supported, loved, and assisted by the whole.

Bringing it all together

We still align with our limited self when we switch from victim to victor. We call upon the power of the ego, which we usually perceive as control and manipulation. Many of us no longer choose to play with this power, at least not consciously. We align ourselves with our True Selves when we move into the role of vehicle, and that is True Power: the power of LOVE. We can Be (both extend and receive) love, and that is the greatest power in the universe. Imagine living a life always aligned with such power. Your life would be fabulous. You would fear nothing, and therefore you would judge nothing.

Understanding and accepting that I am responsible for my life and all its conditions brings us a great gift, for if I create my environment, I can change it! I am powerless as a victim. I am in charge as a victor. God and I are in charge as a vehicle. Wow—what freedom! What power!

With this understanding there is *no blame* and therefore *no pain*. There is only acceptance—I created or attracted what I perceive in my environment, and I will recreate my environment with God as my co-creator, rather than my ego or limited-self. You would *see* a different world overnight if you did this. And if it takes more than overnight, so what? The important point is to move beyond blame into acceptance. Only then can we change our minds about ourselves.

Life as a dance

We have been talking about the process of remembering our true nature. This process seems to take time, because we take time to get past our fear. We greatly fear that we will lose something in this journey back to God, perhaps even ourselves. We thus protect and defend our old ways. It is a step-by-step, inch-by-inch, peeling away layer-by-layer process.

I was counseling someone the other day and I was guided to show her the dance of the process. I stood up and explained to her that it looks like two steps forward and one step back, three steps forward and two steps back, and so on. I found myself dancing across the room. It really was a lot of fun! My cautious steps became very fluid as I moved my body to an unheard rhythm. There were a lot of steps back, but I did make it to the other side of the room.

If we would look at our process in the same way, as a dance and not a tightrope walk, we wouldn't mind our occasional steps back. We could dance to whatever tune and rhythm we wanted. The process can be fun, light, and easy. When we approach this as though we are walking across a tight-rope 500 feet above the ground, though, the journey looks quite perilous. We are cautious, afraid to move for fear that it might be wrong. Instead, we do make unnecessary moves, or repeat old failed decisions, or feel paralyzed and unable to move at all.

I've since incorporated the dance as a playshop exercise. It felt appropriate to play some music and sing during this exercise, and I felt guided to pick a gospel song I wrote to words from Lesson #155 in *A Course in Miracles,* "I will step back and let Him lead the way." As everyone danced it became clear that we can look at the steps back as a way to step back and allow God, our Higher Power, to lead us. We need the steps back for the times when we don't feel on course or connected. They are not backward steps at all, but rather very important parts of the process. They provide an opportunity for our paths to be guided, rather than forced. Because if we did know the way, we would have arrived by now!

Try it! Stand up and walk across your room. One step forward, one step back, two steps forward, one step back, three steps forward, two steps back. Move cautiously going from one side of the room to the other, as though you were walking on a tight rope. Now play with it—let go of the caution and start to dance. Use the same progression of steps, or change them, but feel the joy that comes from dancing through your process rather than trudging. Now imagine dancing your way through each day, through all of your issues, through all of your fears. Facing a fear can actually be fun.

Moving in and out of the feeling

When we align more and more with our Higher Power, a wonderful thing begins to happen. We feel the *presence* of the love of God. This feeling of bliss, serenity, and complete inner peace varies from person to person. Tension, anxiety, and worry are absent. We know that **all** is in Divine order, that something far greater than us is in charge.

Initially, one cannot imagine ever leaving this feeling. It is too glorious a space to leave. This feeling can last for minutes, hours, days, weeks, months. For the vast majority, however, it will not last indefinitely. We usually have difficulty with too much joy in the early stages of the transformational process. Leaving this state of bliss feels like a crash landing at first, disquieting and uncomfortable. Many will question what they did wrong, to leave such peace and joy. The answer is nothing! You did nothing wrong! This is simply part of the process, and as this continues you will move in and out of the direct conscious connected feeling of God's love. Admittedly this is not easy, nor is it much fun. It is quite disconcerting, in fact, because of the extremes of the two feelings: absolute joy and bliss and the so-called "real world." I have heard people say time and time again, "Welcome back to the real world," or after a five-day workshop experience, "I have to go back to the real world." But the **real** world is much closer to bliss and ecstasy. The important thing here is: Do not judge yourself when you feel like you've lost the feeling. Remember, it is just another part of the dance.

I don't know of anyone who did not lose this feeling of connection. Joel Goldsmith, author of dozens of books including the popular *Infinite Way*, felt as though he had lost this connection for a time in the later part of his life. The kindest thing we can do for ourselves when we feel this way is to remember the dance. For a time, we are putting our attention on a step back. Forgiving ourselves for this temporary digression is the quickest way back to bliss. Judging ourselves or God only increases our awareness of discomfort, and the length of time we experience that discomfort.

The Highs, the Lows and eventually the Evens

Patrick has arrived at a point in his life where he lives from day to day in peace. He doesn't experience huge "highs," and he rarely has "lows." He remembers the highs and the lows, the feeling of living on a continual roller coaster, but that was some time ago. He now lives with the "Evens." First the feeling of God's love seems very high, and stepping away from this love feels very low. As we learn to accept this love, though, and accept ourselves, we will become increasingly aware of God's presence and love.

So, enjoy the process! Surrender to your Higher Self and relax—the Universe really is in charge. As we become a vehicle through which love expresses, we will perceive the glorious creation in which we play.

Exercises

1. Read the section *Rules for Decision* in Chapter 30 of *A Course in Miracles* and practice the exercises daily, or...

2. Follow these steps upon waking:

    a. What kind of a day would you like? How would you like to feel today?

    b. Decide to make all decisions with your Higher Power. (It does not matter what you think your Higher Power is at this point.)

    c. Every choice you make during the day is an opportunity to quiet your mind and listen to what you hear or feel would be the best choice. Remember, this is usually the choice that will bring peace.

    d.   When you find yourself feeling conflict (fear) simply say "I must have chosen without my Higher Power" and begin at step a. again.

3.   Repeat the dance exercise discussed earlier. Do this at least once a day for a week. (See how your life becomes a dance, rather than a tightrope walk.)

4.   Find someone willing to do the dance exercise with you. Partner "A" will do the same tightrope walk from the preceding exercise, while Partner "B" guides "A" with such phrases as: "be careful, look out, don't fall, toe the line, watch your step." Notice how this feels to both persons. "A" should go all the way across the room in this manner, being careful while "B" guides, and then the partners should switch roles.

After each partner plays both roles, dance the dance! Throw caution to the wind! Your partner will tell you such things as "go for it, you can do it, you look great, feel free." As you cross the room, dance with your partner, supporting each other with enthusiasm.

Notice how different it feels while being supported with encouragement and messages of joy and freedom. Imagine dancing through each day, through all of your issues, through all of your fears. Facing a fear can be fun!

6

And the Walls Came Tumbling Down

**We hide from God all the while
seeking God. We hide from each
other all the while seeking for our
true love. Let's stop playing hide
and seek.**

"**H**umpty sat on a wall, Humpty Dumpty had a great
fall. All the King's horses and all the King's men
couldn't put Humpty together again." As I begin this chapter, this nursery rhyme keeps running through
my head. I am reminded of the walls of Jericho, and more
recently, the Berlin wall that tumbled down. Walls are coming down all around us—are we afraid that we, like Humpty
Dumpty, will never be put back together again?

Opening to receive

Opening to receive may be the stage in the process of undoing that has been the least talked about. Much emphasis has
been placed on the importance of giving, but in Truth giving
and receiving are the same, even though we kid ourselves
about how open we are to receive. How willing are you to

receive? If you have scarcity in any area of your life, you are resisting the concept of receiving. How easy is it for you to receive gifts from others? Do you allow friends to take you out to lunch, or do you always pay? Do you accept compliments, or reject them with such answers as "Oh, no not really," or "I'm not really that great." Do you accept gifts easily on your birthday? How easy is it for you to receive a hug— a full body hug where you allow yourself physical and emotional contact with the other person? Be honest with yourself. How willing are you to be in an intimate relationship? How willing are you to share your entire self, your hopes, your dreams, your fears, your beliefs about yourself? How willing are you to let others in? How willing are you to receive?

I had an interesting telephone conversation with my mother a couple of years ago. It was quite late at night and I wanted to go to bed, but I felt obligated to call her, since I was leaving on a trip the next day. You can imagine that I was not in the most open and willing state of mind at that moment. On top of that my mom was overly concerned with something that she thought I was doing, or not doing, with my husband. I explained to her that I did not understand her point, and that I didn't want to talk with her while she was in such a state. I told her good night and hung up.

I immediately went to bed and meditated for a while. A peaceful voice within asked me to look at my life and discover when I am happiest. That was easy; I am happiest when I work: teach, sing, speak, counsel, and go on tour. I was asked to understand why. That was easy, too. I don't have any walls when I work; I don't try to protect myself, my time, or my energy, and I usually am in a constant state of bliss. I allow energy to flow through me; I am open and vulnerable, and I am always happy. I feel invulnerable because of my choice for vulnerability.

Setting limits and boundaries

I often put up walls when I am not working, around people that I know the best: my mom, my husband, and my closest friends. This might sound very strange that I would protect myself from those closest to me and not from "strangers." Why do I need to erect these walls? Because I often didn't take care of myself in the past. These walls "protect" my time, my space, and my energy. But I did this because I was not setting limits and boundaries for myself. I didn't take a nap when I visited my mom, because I wanted to be nice, for example. I wasn't doing those things that keep me in balance, centered, and energized, and I would put up walls to protect myself from others. I used all sorts of excuses for why I couldn't meditate or exercise, but the fact is that I wasn't taking care of myself. I can't judge myself for this. Most of us were never taught to take care of ourselves, and instead were taught to be caretakers for others. We were not taught limits and boundaries, and thus building walls has become automatic. The only way I know they exist is that they have become increasingly uncomfortable.

I set a limit in the above conversation with my mother. I gave her the message that I didn't want to talk to her while she exhibited obsessive behavior. In fact, we had a great conversation the next day about her fears, my meditation of the previous night, the understanding of my walls against her, and how we could support each other in creating an even healthier relationship.

The truth is, these **walls don't protect**. They bring tension, exhaustion, and illness, and only continue the feeling of separation. The more we keep them up the more separated we feel.

Remember what it was like when you fell in love? No walls! You were eager to know this person, and neither person could do any wrong. All was glorious. You were relating to the perfection of the person. You were in love with his/

her True Self. Then, little by little, you judged your partner ever so slightly—little things, like the way he or she ate, or squeezed the toothpaste, or kept house. But what happens when you judge? The walls go up! They have to. The moment that we judge, we must defend ourselves, and up go the walls.

Why we defend ourselves

We attack when we judge, and we protect and defend ourselves against an expected counter-attack by putting up our walls. It is really exhausting, when you think about it. I have an unlimited supply of energy when I am working, but the moment I protect or judge, I feel tired. It takes energy to keep up the walls. A client of mine compared it to the shields on Star Trek's Starship Enterprise. The Enterprise raises its shields when it expects to be attacked. These shields take energy, diverting power from other areas in the ship.

Protecting ourselves from Love

It is not our natural state to protect ourselves from one another, since we really are protecting ourselves from God as well. We are all the same energy, and we can easily see that we are protecting ourselves from Love.

This experience in meditation was extremely liberating, and I made the commitment to take the walls down and never put them back up. They have gone up a few times since that commitment, but other remarkable experiences have happened as well. Within days of this conversation with my mom I was scheduled to give a talk. Since my talks usually flow from experience, I shared the above conversation and my understanding of these walls. During the talk I felt an inner urge to allow myself to receive the audience's love. The feeling was overwhelming; I cannot explain it in words. I couldn't talk, tears were flowing from my eyes, and I felt so full that I couldn't contain it; I gave it back. I sent love to each and every person in the congregation. Within moments, almost everyone in the room was crying, and without words everyone knew what was occurring. Love was flowing from everyone in the room to everyone else in the room. Finally, I was able to read a section from *A Course in Miracles* as I had planned, crying the entire time. For a few minutes, we all let down our walls and experienced our oneness.

I visited a different organization two weeks later, and I felt the same flow of love even before I stood up. I knew I had a choice—to stay open and receive this love, or to turn it down, and I knew that I had been given this choice many times before. On prior occasions I would suppress this feeling before I spoke, because I wanted to be in control. After all, I am a professional speaker, and it is not appropriate to cry in front of all these people! This time however, I didn't turn it down. I was crying when I stood up, and my talk began with words that my ego believed came out of left field. Having recently tasted oneness, however, I allowed myself to receive at this new level once again, and it was awesome. Again, there are no words. The talk felt different from my point of view. I did not feel "in charge" of what was being said, or how it was being said. The feedback was incredible, however. I received a standing ovation. A group of women came up to me after the service, and one said: "All this time I thought I was protecting myself from others' judgments and fears and limited awareness, and all the time what I have been protecting myself from is their LOVE." Ah, yes! That is indeed what we have been doing. We made up the notion that the walls protect us from one another's egos, when in fact we use the walls to maintain the separation, protecting ourselves from one another's love.

The next day in counseling, a client shared the following realization: "When we meditate, we believe that we are opening ourselves to feel God's love. Then we go out into the world and do not allow ourselves to feel each other's love. **But**, God's love and your love is the same love, because that is what we are: God's love. So, if I close myself off from your love, I am in that same moment closing myself off from God's love. I can't open to God and stay closed to my brothers and sisters. I must open myself to both, or I am not open to either. If we have walls up around each other, we also are walling ourselves off from God. It is a great way to keep both the idea and the feeling of separation going."

Another client shared with me that I had given him one of the greatest gifts he had ever received during that Sunday talk. I was taken aback by this comment. He said, "I was sitting in the back of the room consciously sending you as much love as I could. We had eye contact and I saw you take in my love, feel it, and then give it back to me. I don't remember when anyone has allowed herself to receive that much love from me. It was a great gift. Thank you." We are starving for love. We perceive that the planet is starving for love. And yet, love is all around us, within us, being given to us all the time. But we believe that there is something we must do to find this love. There **is** something we must do— allow the walls to come down. That's all.

I remember the first time that I felt this oneness. I was in Sonoma, California, eating lunch at a restaurant across from the Sonoma Mission Inn. My friend, Peter, and I were sitting across from each other eating, when suddenly I knew and felt that everyone in the room was connected to me, with no barriers. We were One. It was incredible. I looked around the room and saw how we were all the same. I could see the differences: some people were large; others were small; one man was in a wheelchair; some were old, others young. These differences really didn't matter though. I felt an expanded awareness, as though I was as big as the room and we were all in touch with one another. No words can describe this, but the experience had a very large impact. My later experiences were more intense, I suppose, because I allowed in more love. I sense that I have just opened up a crack, but that I will become accustomed to this much love. The crack will open a bit more, and a bit more, until I am fully ready to feel the love that is the truth of who I am.

I must be a willing participant in the dismantling of my walls. I must make a 100% commitment to the release of the walls that protect me from your love. I cannot judge, because the moment I do, the walls will go up again. I cannot judge you, but equally important, I cannot judge myself. We keep the walls in part because we do not feel worthy of this love. Only when we allow the walls to come down, however, can we understand that we are worthy of this tremendous love that we all are. It takes courage and willingness to open that crack a little. Eventually we will not fear the tremendous love that we all really want to give and receive.

Other gifts

As a result of my dismantling process, I have not been attracting as many "lessons" as I have in the past. I do not find myself embroiled in as many dramas, and when a potential problem does arise, I find myself choosing whether or not to engage in the game. If I do, I usually end the drama within a short time, because it is clear that the drama, the game, the engagement always begins in my mind, and that is where it will stop. It is always my choice to engage or not, and the game is always played in my mind. It is a choice for peace or ego—it always comes back to that. Simple, isn't it?

Other side benefits

Another interesting side benefit involves my relationship with animals. During this time, we had two absolutely marvelous cats, Pooh Bah and Katisha, both of which were wonderful hunters. Our cats brought their gifts to us unharmed once I began opening to receive more. Pooh Bah and Katisha both brought birds into the house; the birds were never wounded, although I am sure they must have been a bit traumatized. These birds initially would fly around the house trying to get out, and eventually I would catch them and set them free. Later, however, once I got the cats out, the birds would sit calmly, allowing me to pick them up and put them outside, where they flew away. The birds seemed to trust me. I must admit that I have wanted to be like St. Francis with the animals ever since I was a little girl, but this seems to demonstrate that the love I was feeling was transmitted to the birds.

In addition, those in my immediate family are getting through their issues with greater ease and grace. This love is catching! The more I allow myself to feel the receiving and sending of it, the more those around me feel it. This has a dramatic effect in everyone's life. It takes practice and constant reminders to keep the walls down, however. Walls were a constant part of my everyday life, and my limited self is still very attached to them. I must ask for daily assistance in not putting them up again, and I also must consciously practice sending and receiving this love during my daily activities. Otherwise, I find myself slipping back into old unconscious patterns that no longer serve and are no longer comfortable. The rewards, however, are beyond words and are worth the conscious commitment and practice.

Exercises

1. From whom do you protect yourself in your life? Make
    a list of these people and let your walls down with at
    least two of them. Consciously ask for guidance and
    assistance from your True Self in how to do this, and
    make a 100% commitment to release the protective
    walls. Consciously choose to receive love from these
    people, remembering that they too are an extension of
    God's perfect and safe love. Allow love to flow in a
    circular pattern from them to you and back. Don't
    explain what you are doing; just do it, and do not judge
    the process. That will simply bring back the walls.

2. Make yourself three-by-five cards, or post'em notes at
    home, in your car, and at your workplace to assist you
    in remembering your choice to receive and experience
    the truth of what you are: Love. In other words, do
    whatever it takes!

7

Man Plans & God Laughs

or

How Great Expectations Create Great Disappointments

How many of you make plans? Do you plan your day, or your week? Do you make a year plan, a five-year plan? How about a life plan?

Most of us were taught to make plans. Goal-setting books teach us to plan. Growing up, we may have been told that "We must plan for our future." Planning is something we are encouraged to do, and many of us are quite good at it. We plan such things as our careers, our vacations, our retirements, how much income we are going to earn, and by what age. Quite often I have heard from people planning a relationship that just started. A woman once called me to share that she had just met a wonderful man over the weekend. She described him in great detail and asked whether he would be an appropriate person for her to marry! As ridiculous as that may sound, I am sure that we have all entertained such ideas and based our plans on equally insufficient data.

I also observe people planning the lives of their children. This is not so prevalent today, but not so long ago parents picked the colleges, and often the field of study for their offspring before they were born. The destiny of a child often was determined by the profession, status, and income of the parents: the child of a merchant would inherit the father's business, and a farmer's son would grow up to be a farmer. Our lives today are not so dictated by our parents' status, I imagine this may lead many parents to create goals and expectations for their children.

Planning in and of itself is neutral; neither good nor bad. Our attitude and expectations about plans causes us peace or discomfort. Are you disappointed if your plans don't work out? Do you feel that you did not plan well enough, or that *you* are not good enough? If your children do not desire to fulfill your plans for them, do you feel that they let you down? Do you feel God didn't hear you, or let you down? Do you ever blame God or others when your plans don't work out? If you feel any of the above, be aware that you are attached to your plans!

Plans appear to be necessary in my line of work. I agree upon a time and place for a talk and playshop with organizations. Sometimes these are planned a year in advance, and a tour is planned around my engagements.

Last year my husband and I had a marvelous plan. In early May we embarked upon a two month cross-country tour, followed by a month rest at Lake Tahoe, a tour of Seattle during August, and four months in France for a house exchange with a French family. Sounds like a marvelous plan, doesn't it? All went according to plan until the second day of our vacation at Lake Tahoe. Patrick and I love to look at Open Houses. We get ideas for decorating and remodeling, and look at areas where we might move someday. Patrick and I had pretty much settled on Lake Tahoe as our ultimate destination, but the time wasn't right. After all, we had not yet sold our home in Virginia, and our four-month house exchange began in September. But on the second day of our vacation my mom bought a Tahoe newspaper, which included a section on properties for sale. One ad, entitled "**Fore-closure**," included a picture of an outstanding view and said "price reduced $30,000." There were very few homes with that view, so for the fun of it I said "Let's go find the house." We got in our car and drove all of one and one-half blocks. We saw a "For Sale" sign, walked around to the back yard, and there was the **view**! The house was vacant, so we peered in the windows and discovered that the back door was open. We went in. The interior was quite unique, with soaring ceilings, lots of windows, a fabulous kitchen, and a bathroom with a three-by-six foot tiled Jacuzzi tub. Patrick was in love! I was interested, but the timing didn't fit our plans, and there were those rust-colored rugs. We walked over to the house that evening to look at it again. We found that it had recessed lighting in the soaring ceilings—it really was quite dramatic. Pamela was in love!

I realized the next day that there was coincidence attached to this house. The year before, my mother and I had rented the same townhouse we were currently renting. I have a four-person raft that I love to row, and one day that year I rowed out into the lake from our rented townhouse and over to the main homeowner's section. I tied my raft to a dock (which was sinking) in back of a rundown and deserted house, walked back to our townhouse, and invited my mom for a ride in the raft. That was the same house that, one year later almost to the day, we now loved.

After viewing the house for a third time, we decided it really was perfect for us. The price was an incredible bargain, and after meditating on the decision we wrote up an offer. One of four offers to come in that weekend (July 4th), ours was accepted. One phone call later to a friend to arrange financing, we were in escrow—so much for our other plans. Good-bye to a month's vacation, not to mention four months in France.

The next month we took care of all the details involved in buying a house: inspections, repairs, title searches, funding. Not exactly what I had expected on my vacation. During this month, I experienced feelings ranging from joy, excitement, and gratitude to frustration, anger, and resentment. I lost my feelings of joy about the new house whenever I focused on not getting my desperately needed vacation. Patrick had to go East for a couple of weeks, leaving all the preparations to me. I also felt resentful about that.

A plan is an expectation

I began to understand during this process that making a plan is the same as having an expectation. Why make a plan if you do not expect it to happen? I expected to have a vacation. I expected to go to France for four months. The French family expected to come to our house in Virginia for four months. (We found another exchange family in Virginia for them.)

Being attached to the plan is the issue, not the plan itself. Attachment to a plan causes disappointment, anger, and resentment when the plan does not work. Our expectation of the plan's success causes our problems, not the plan itself. In Chapter Five we discussed making every decision with our Higher Power; we also must release to our Higher Power each and every expectation we have around our plans and decisions.

An expectation is a premeditated resentment

Many in 12-step programs define an expectation as a "premeditated resentment." There is always a strong reaction every time I share this definition with a group. If we equate planning with expectations, it becomes crystal clear that we need to release our attachment to our plans. If we don't, we can be assured that we will experience a resentment.

I thought a lot about expectations on a recent trip to the East Coast. We had rented our Virginia home for the four months preceding the house exchange in France. The tenants called us a couple of weeks before our purchase of the house at Tahoe and asked if we were certain of our trip to France, because they very much wanted to continue to rent our Virginia home. Fortune thus smiled upon us again. They had rented the house furnished, including most of our personal belongings. Since our new house was unfurnished we discussed coming back to get our belongings, which was perfectly acceptable to them. We arrived back in Virginia in early September, after closing escrow on our Tahoe home. Our tenants said that they had packed up our entire kitchen, and placed all our paintings in boxes they had used for moving their items from California; everything was ready for us to pick up. Well... upon arriving, I found that the paintings were stuffed in boxes without padding, in one case with six paintings stuffed into one box. I expected that everything would be packed the way I would pack, but instead I repacked all of the paintings and all of the kitchen boxes.

I believe that having expectations is one of our most successful methods of creating pain for ourselves. We expect others to be how we want them to be, to do what we want them to do in the way we want. When they don't, we feel let down, angry, disappointed, and even resentful. Take a moment and think about this. Do you have expectations, positive or negative, about your employees or your employer? Do you have expectations of your children, your mate, your minister, or your President? In all honesty, don't we have expectations about just about everyone in our lives? You can even extend this to "inanimate" objects—your car, your computer, your furnace, your washer and dryer.

In my travels to various spiritual communities throughout the United States, I often arrive at a church that is undergoing a ministerial change: the minister is about to leave, the congregation is currently without a minister, or a new minister has been recently hired. This process is extremely informative. Congregation members become very attached to their ministers, and the expectations are enormous when someone new arrives. This causes pain and disappointment or frustration for both the members and the new minister. The expectations create chaos within the church. In all cases, some members leave, sometimes as much as half the congregation. In some cases, the minister is asked to leave after a short time. The members have become accustomed to the previous minister, and often they have determined in their mind how they want their new minister to be.

Paramahansa Yogananda describes in *Autobiography of a Yogi* a meeting he had scheduled with his guru. He arrived for this meeting approximately three days late, and he was filled with trepidation over what his guru would say to him and how he would feel. His guru replied:

> **"I do not expect anything from others, so their actions cannot be in opposition to wishes of mine. I would not use you for my own ends. I am happy only in your own true happiness."** [1]

Imagine not having expectations. We would experience no disappointments if we did not have expectations. We would no longer be concerned about whether things will work out as planned. We could plan, and make another plan when and if needed.

To go back to "our plan," we had decided to rent a U-Haul truck in Virginia, take some of our furniture, and tow our car back home. But our tenants informed us that they had rented the house "furnished," and that we must have misunderstood when they said we could take anything we wanted, because they meant only personal items such as cookware. So we made a new plan. We would rent a five-by-eight trailer and tow it across the country with our Suburu.

But the SVX was not suited for towing. No problem—we knew that something else would become available. Sure enough our friend Thomas volunteered to tow the trailer across the country with his Toyota truck. GREAT! We rented the trailer and filled it to capacity. Thomas hitched it up to his truck, and off we went. Two miles later Thomas stopped and informed us that his Toyota was not up to the job. So we needed yet another plan.

An expectation usually comes from fear

During this entire episode, I wondered about the planning. Do we need to plan? Are plans helpful? *A Course in Miracles* states that a healed mind does not plan. The Universe already knows what our needs are, and its resources are always available to us. Once, again, though, I discovered that it is not the planning that causes stress; instead, it is the expectations we have about the plans. These events taught me that we are usually coming from a place of fear whenever we have an expectation.

A Course in Miracles teaches that we either experience love and extend it to others, or we live in a state of fear. All our thoughts, actions, and feelings are determined by whether we are feeling love or feeling fear. When we have expectations, we want something to turn out a certain way, or someone to fill a certain role for us. Actually, we are trying to control our reality and our environment. Coming from an open heart does not coincide with having expectations, for I am conditionally loving and conditionally accepting when I expect anyone to be a certain way for me. If I expect my plans to work out, I am attempting to manipulate and control my environment and everyone around me.

We had the opportunity to trust the Universe (extend love) or go into fear every time our plans fell apart on our move. How would we get our stuff across the country? What would we do about furniture? We have a choice each and every time our plans (expectations) don't work out: love or fear, trust or control?

I gave a playshop in Seattle last August. One of the participants was very vocal. He commented on almost every idea that we discussed. He pushed a lot of buttons for people, which made him a wonderful stimulant for the group. He shared a story about a recent series of relationships. He had been in a relationship and he left it. No sooner had he closed the door on one then another came along. He left that relationship, but immediately attracted another, and then another, until he said "OK, God—enough! When I want a relationship I will tell you who, when, where, and how!"

I sat there and smiled. I was really amused. I remember talking to God like that. I remember thinking that I knew what was best for me. I remember telling God "who, when, where and how, or what, when, where and how." I even remember bargaining with God. Have you ever done that? "I'll do this if you give me (fill in the blank)." I discovered ten years ago that I often received what I told the Universe I wanted, and often it was not what I wanted because it didn't make me **happy**! It brought lessons, but it didn't make me happy. So I kept learning lessons, until I realized that maybe, just maybe, the Universe might know what I wanted more than I did.

I've given my life, my wants, my needs, and my plans to God. I've learned not to be attached to my plans. The opportunity in Virginia was to know, really know, that this all was in perfect order. We were not victims of our tenants, or Thomas, or anyone, and nothing was going wrong—we just needed to be open to what was best for all concerned. We bought a Ford Bronco and towed the trailer with that. My husband loves it, and it is a perfect vehicle for Tahoe.

When we let go of our attachments to how, what, who, when, and where, leaving the Universe in charge, we can truly feel free and happy. When we allow our Higher Power to move through us and others, expecting only that the Universe will be in charge, we will understand that Perfect Order is real and we will relax into this flow of love.

The Gifts

What are the gifts that we receive when we let go of expectations?

1. Present Time. We stay in present time, which is the only place where we feel a conscious connection to Source. (Please refer to the Chapter Eight.) We are not worried about the future and its limitless possibilities.

2. Freedom. We allow others to be who they naturally are. We do not demand others to be what we want them to be, or do what we want them to do. We extend to them the gift of freedom to be and to do whatever they desire, which allows us to experience this freedom as well.

3. No disappointments. We are open to receive whatever is for our highest good, without judgment. This allows us to attract to ourselves much more than we might have planned. We do not block ourselves from receiving the abundance of the Universe.

4. Spontaneity. We give ourselves the freedom to change our minds without being locked into a specific plan.

5. No resentments. No expectations = no resentments!

6. Divine order. When we witness events without judgment, we understand and experience the perfect order of the Universe.

7. Happiness is the result.

Further insight: Why our plans fail

Concurrently while writing this chapter, I also was reading the latest book by Paul Ferrini, *Love Without Conditions.* In his chapter "Power and Mastery," he discusses the dynamics that occur when *"you commit yourself to a specific course of action,"* [2] i.e., make a plan.

He explains that we create a plan at the level of the mind that is the source of incredible power. He goes on:

> *" Power exists as potential. As soon as it manifests outwardly, as force, it must overcome the resistance of its environment. It is therefore weakened. Power remains strongest when it is held in trust and not outwardly expressed...*
>
> *" The conceptual mind expects linear results from every action taken. Yet linear results are rare. As soon as a force meets a resistance, its course is altered. It moves up, down, or around the obstruction. Often it is deflected from its original trajectory.*
>
> *" In spite of this, all your planning anticipates linear outcomes. It is no wonder that you are disappointed so often."* [3]

In other words, we create a plan in our mind. The moment that we put our plan into action, it is met with the resistance of third-dimensional reality (form) and is almost always changed through this interaction. This is why our plans do not work with regularity.

Conflicting goals within the same plan

In addition, most of our plans are made without the assistance of our Higher Power, without consulting the Universe. Lesson 24 in the workbook of *A Course in Miracles*, entitled *"I do not perceive my own best interests"* states:

> *" In no situation that arises do you realize the outcome that would make you happy. Therefore, you have no guide to appropriate action, and no way of judging the result... It is inevitable, then, that you will not serve your own best interests."*[4]

The lesson then goes on to explain that, in most cases, if you carefully examined your goals and plans, you would

> *" quickly realize that you have a number of goals in mind as part of the desired outcome, and also that these goals are on different levels and often conflict."*[5]

For instance, a writer may have a goal of publishing a best-selling book but at the same time may have a goal to remain unknown. A person may have the goal of getting into a relationship, but also wants to protect his space, fearing intimacy. Quite often you desire conflicting outcomes from your plans. How, then, do you expect the plan to work out as "planned?"

Didn't I learn this already?

Have you discovered that you keep attracting to yourself the same lessons or opportunities over and over again? Have you ever heard someone else say "I thought that I already learned this one?" I often have wondered why this is so.

As we previously discussed, our ego knows how to upset us. It knows the buttons to push and the events that take us out of a peaceful state.

We also tend to make decisions and formulate plans from the level of the ego, rather than with God—in other words, from a needy or fearful position. Have you ever heard that you will have to make a decision again if you make it based in fear? Any plan or decision made from the level of the ego is based in guilt and fear, and it will be recycled; the decision will need to be repeated. How could we possibly perceive our own best interests when we make a decision from a place of fear? Only when we make our decisions and our plans with assistance from our Higher Power are they made in love and without expectations.

Paul Ferrini states:

" Since most decisions are ill-taken they tend to be recycled. They are brought into circular orbit by guilt. Guilt is like a magnetic field that keeps each decision open to constant doubt and reinterpretation. Guilt brings all actions home, offering the same choice over and over in different situations."[6]

In Chapter Five we discussed the advisability of making all decisions with our Higher Power, with God. Making a plan is the same as making a decision; one therefore can see the necessity of making all plans with our Higher Power. In that way, we are more likely to make a plan based in love, rather than fear, and we are less likely to repeat the same lessons over and over again.

Recently, a client and I were working with this concept. Virginia had recently decided to break off a relationship because she did not feel that she had the time to devote to it. She has a full-time job, grown children, grandchildren, and is starting a new career in a multi-level company. Her decision was based on the idea of "lack," in this case a lack of time. I reminded her that any decision based in fear (lack) must be recycled. As we talked a wonderful new perception came to both of us. Most of us blame ourselves when we ask the question "Didn't I do this one before?" Instead, we should realize that we have the opportunity to choose again. Every decision we made out of a sense of fear or guilt can be changed. Virginia thus decided to look at time and relationship in a different way. She realized that a relationship can actually support her, rather than take from her, and she will contact this man so that he can come back into her life in a new and abundant way.

We can rejoice over the fact that our old decisions based upon fear must be repeated. This time we can choose to make our decisions and our plans from the space of love, with the assistance of our Higher Power.

How to plan

Before making any plans, it is preferable to enter into a state of prayer or meditation and communication with your Higher Power. Concentrate on the plan and watch it unfold within your mind. Ask for affirmation on making the plan, changing the plan, or discarding the plan. Ask for anyone who might be involved in the plan to give you input during this prayer time. Remember, we are all connected at the level of mind, and we can communicate with each other at any time.

Exercises

1. Every morning dedicate your life to God. Give God your plans in this dedication and ask for release from expectations.

2. Listen to your Higher Power. Be still, be quiet and listen. Be open to receiving God's plan.

3. Release expectations about EVERYTHING:

    — about hearing God's voice;

    — about your plans;

— about God's plans;

— about others in your life, how they are supposed to be, what they are supposed to do, and how they are supposed to do it.

4. Remember, God's will for you is only happiness. When you find you are not happy, or things seem to hurt, say this: "God's will for me is happiness and I accept God's will for me today. Thank you!"

5. Before taking action on a plan or goal, place yourself in a quiet state of mind. Focus on your breath. Bring this plan or goal into as much focus as you can.

This can be any plan or goal: buying a house, a project at work, taking a vacation, or something to do with a relationship. Pick a plan that includes at least one other person. Bring each person into your thoughts and ask them for feedback concerning the plan. Listen carefully, and let go of any expectations that you might have. Then, watch the action unfold as you discuss various possibilities.

Remain in this state of awareness and look at all the goals you hold about this plan. Are there any conflicting goals within the plan? Be amused by this, but recognize that conflicting goals are difficult to achieve.

8

Time Management

T his topic amuses me, because even though many of us give a lot of power to it, it isn't even real: TIME. There are classes given on time management, books written about how to make the best use of time, seminars given on how to not waste time, and generally lots of thought devoted to time. We spend a great deal of time thinking about time. How many of us have our Day Timers with us all the time?

What is this thing called time? Simply expressed, time is another ego mechanism that diverts, distracts, and annoys us. Its allure diverts us from our primary focus of the truth that we are the sons and daughters of an unlimited, abundant, and all-sufficient universe.

That's the bad news. We did it again. We made up something else with which to punish ourselves. Let's focus on how we can use time to our advantage. Once again, let's change our perception.

Deepak Chopra states in his book *Unconditional Life*: "*I have done my best to provide convincing proof that reality is everyone's personal creation.*"[1] He continues with quotes from a guru who admonishes his students:

> "*You believe that you live in the world, when in fact the world lives in you.*"[2]

" Once you realize that the world is your own projection, you will be free of it... Everything existing around you is painted on the screen of your consciousness.

" The picture you see may be ugly or beautiful, but in either case you are not bound by it. Rest assured, there is no one who has forced it on you. You are trapped only because of your habit of mistaking the imaginary for the real."[3]

We could apply these all-encompassing statements about life and Truth, to any aspect of our lives. Let's look at the subject of time. Each of us has a personal perception of time. For some of us it moves quickly, while for others it drags on forever. This can change from day to day, depending upon our situation and our activities. I am intrigued by the quote: "You are trapped only because of your habit..."

How many of us have felt trapped by time? Time is not outside of you, but rather is inside of your mind; you determine its power, and whether or not you choose to be its "victim." I automatically become time's victim when I believe time is outside of me. I become the world's victim when I see it as outside of myself. I am money's victim when I see money as outside of myself. This is true with relationships, health, careers, and even God.

I've had clients tell me "I always have just enough money." So guess what they had—*just enough* money. That can be a very stressful way to live. I suggested that they change from "I always have just enough money " to "I always have more than enough money." This had worked for me. I then examined my belief about time, and sure enough my affirmation concerning time was "I never have enough." Every time I said this I was affirming that as the truth and sending this message to my consciousness. I never felt as if I had enough time.

Dr. Chopra in his "Magical Mind, Magical Body" tape series relates stories of people who live in a state of fear because they don't believe they have enough time. Their belief became a self-fulfilling prophecy because they died at an early age. So I changed my affirmation to say: "I always have more than enough time to do everything that I want to do." This allows me to relax, and I usually get things done more efficiently and at a higher level of quality than when I feel under the gun.

In an *On Course* article called "The Time Trap," Jon Mundy writes that time is relative. It can slow down and it can speed up. Einstein's secretary once asked him to explain to her the theory of relativity and he replied: *'Two hours with a beautiful woman seems like two minutes. Two minutes on a hot stove seems like two hours. That is relativity.'*[4]

So we have different beliefs about time. Some of us believe it is limited, while others believe there is an abundance of it; since we also believe time is relative, we can hold both of the above beliefs depending upon our current activity. Whether time is moving slowly or quickly is determined only by *your* belief.

One belief I inherited from my grandmother is that "the older you get, the faster time goes." I can relate to that—the years do seem to go by more quickly. Others have a new idea about time: "Celestial speedup." I'm not sure I know exactly what that means, but I do know that the ego is *using* this belief system as well, and I can choose to buy into it or not!

I love reading books and watching movies about science fiction. How many *Star Trek* movies or episodes deal with time and time travel? We are intrigued by time, especially as we approach the year 2000. Every thousand years "dooms-day" prophecies tell us what we must do, or not do, because "time is running out." That's a cheerful thought. Most of these prophecies are filled with fearful predictions that California will fall into the ocean, Phoenix will be beach property on the Pacific Ocean, and so on. A recent article in the *Sacramento Bee* newspaper claimed that a Greek priest made a mathematical error concerning the birth date of Jesus. The article suggests that new discoveries point to the birth of Jesus in the year 6 B.C., which would mean that we have already past the millennium. OOPS!

NOW

As John Mundy points out:

" **A Course in Miracles** *says that "now" is as close as we can get to eternity. But we keep missing now because we keep falling back into time or projecting ourselves forward into the future and missing the present."* [4]

Most mystical teachings emphasize the importance of focusing on the present. Since time is relative, the only actual time we have for our use is the now.

Another widely used time phrase is "**One day at a time**." For the newly sober alcoholic, this is an invaluable gift. We all can do something for a day, or an hour, or perhaps just a minute, but when we focus on doing, or not doing, something for the rest of our lives, it takes on enormous proportions. A newly sober alcoholic can be overwhelmed by the thought of not drinking for the rest of his/her life. Most of us can handle one day at a time, though, no matter what the circumstance.

When we focus on "One day at a time" we can stay present in this moment, in what we call "now." This is a very powerful place to have our awareness. Several years ago during meditation I was given the following analogy: I was traveling on a rapid transit train. The train stopped and I disembarked. I found myself in a vast expanse of desert. To my right was a large billboard with the words: "This is the future;" beyond this billboard stretched barren desert for miles and miles. To my left was another large billboard with the words: "This is the past," and beyond this lay barren desert for miles and miles as well. I was then directed to look back at the train, which was traveling on an electric rail. I was told: "When you are in the train, you are in the present, and the present is the only time when you will truly feel empowered and in conscious connection with God." This was an excellent metaphor for me because the train was traveling by means of electricity. While I am in the train (the present), I have the use of its power, but the moment that I step out of the train I leave my source of power and enter the barren and lifeless desert (the past or the future).

When I obsess on the past, I start feeling guilty about my life, and when I focus on the future, I may begin experiencing fear. Neither of these feelings results in empowerment. *Now* is a very safe place to be. When I focus on it, I rarely fear anything and I usually don't feel guilty. My power is in the *now*, and I am able to do whatever is at hand. (I am currently planning a future tour and leaving the final result to my Higher Power.)

Personal history also deals with the past. Kirshnamurti in his lectures often stated that the worst asset that a human being has is his/her memory. When we first meet someone,

they have no history and we see them "for the first time."
The next time we meet, we remember things about them—
our last conversation, their job, their health, the status of their
relationship. As time goes on, we learn more and more and
we create for them a history, which we bring every time we
see them. We stop seeing them from a fresh perspective, and
we expect them to act as they have in the past. This freezes
them in our mind. They may have dramatically changed their
feeling about themselves, but we may not observe this change
because we still view them as the same person they were the
last time we saw them.

The truth is that we created time; In fact, we are timeless.
We are eternal. Even though we live in a world that believes
in time and all its limitations, we are not bound by this belief. The world is inside of you. It is in your mind. You control time in your reality.

Exercises

1. What is your perception of time? Ask yourself the following questions and record the answers in your journal.

   a) Do you believe that you do not have enough time?

   b) Do you cram many activities in your life because you feel that there is so much you need to do?"

   c) Do you feel compelled to DO? Do you give yourself self time to just BE? (You might remind yourself that you are a "human being" and not a "human doing.")

   d) Do you have time during your day to relax? And when you do relax, do you have any energy, or are you too exhausted to play?

2. Decide how you would like time to exist in your life. Consciously choose to have *more* than enough time.

3. Create a positive affirmation that supports your decision in exercise #2. Commit to this affirmation.

4. Examine your activities and determine if you keep yourself too busy for self-nurturing. Remember, playing and relaxing are NOT wastes of time.

9

Meditation

"Meditation is a mind filled with love, without conflict."

—Tom Carpenter

As I write this, tomorrow is Independence Day in the United States, and I feel a need to breakout, move, leave... something. It is my first summer on the East Coast, which is everything everyone said it would be: hot and humid. Words did not do it justice, no matter how much people told me about it. You can't explain it, you must feel it.

How true that statement is, especially in relation to such concepts as forgiveness, oneness, union, ecstasy, and meditation. It can be talked about, individuals and groups can banter about ideas, but until it is felt, it cannot be not fully understood. East Coast summers now have a color, flavor, touch, smell, and taste to me, and I had to "Be there" to experience it no matter how much others discussed it.

Indeed, this has been my experience with meditation and forgiveness. You have to "Be there." You know when you reach a state of forgiveness. You feel it. A whole new world opens for you. Your past changes, and you know in your heart that the person whom you forgave was actually your teacher, a person who entered your life as a precious gift.

Meditation is a horse of a different color. One rarely experiences a blissful state of union when first practicing meditation. More likely, a person is unaware of meditating. Much is expected of this "mystical art," but in practice it is extremely simple, and for many not very dramatic. Although one can break through into a different realm when one first starts to meditate, this is not really to be expected. If it does happen, it usually occurs only once or twice.

I remember one afternoon during my first month of practicing this elusive art. I was catapulted into another dimension. I was "taken" somewhere that looked and felt like some near-death experiences. There was a bright light; it was warm, safe, and unbelievably loving. I lost all sense of my physical body, feeling a joining of minds that was positively exquisite. I maintained a sense of my identity, but at the same time experienced a oneness with all other "Beings" around me. It felt like what I imagine heaven will feel. I do not know how long this meditation lasted. What I do know is that I did not want to come back to my body. I resisted, I pleaded, I begged not to come back. When I found myself back in my room, I sobbed uncontrollably for what seemed like a very long time. This was an amazingly intense experience, one that I did not duplicate for many years. Afterwards the first question I had was why? Why did I have to come back? Next I asked: why did I ever come here (Earth) in the first place?

How do we meditate? I think Deepak Chopra in his book *Unconditional Life* puts it better than anyone I have heard or read:

> *"When I sit down to meditate, my inner experience can best be described by what I am not doing: I am not focusing my mind or contemplating any idea. I am not in*

a spiritual or introspective mood...
The best answer is that I am just
not doing: I am engaged in getting
the normal activity of the mind to
turn into silence, but without
coercing it to do so. I am getting
past the inner noise of thoughts
and feelings in order to reveal what
the silent witness inside me is
really like."[2]

I suppose that many of us have a tremendous experience early in our practice of meditation, just so we'll stick with it. These exciting experiences are equally rare, and, in any event are not the point of meditating. The most important part of meditating is that we **do it**, that we set aside a certain time each day to practice Being. It seems funny that we need to practice most what we inherently are, always have been, and always will be: "Being." "Doing" at which we are so accomplished, has nothing to do with what we are. This is one of the reasons we think we need to **do** something when we meditate. The whole point is to *not* do anything during this time. Guided meditations, aura-cleansing activities, and other spiritual techniques are fine, fun, and can be highly beneficial. (There are several in this book.) But are they meditation? No. Meditation is simply *not doing*.

Purpose

The purpose of meditation is for us to touch into the world of non-form, rather than the external world. It is a time to Be rather than Do, and it allows us to move beyond the world of form into the world of creation. If that isn't enticing, I don't know what is!

Meditation is a practice which can be very frustrating for those impatient people like myself who want instantaneous results. And, as that implies, it takes practice to achieve still-ness of mind, a state of being, rather than doing. I wish I could give you a box labeled "Instant Meditation" like in-stant pudding: add milk, stir and *voila*:...but that is not my experience. **The practice is the whole point.** It really doesn't matter how good you judge your meditation to have been. The only really important thing is that you do it.

As I travel giving playshops, I often ask those in the group how many meditate on a regular basis. According to the show of hands, only a small percentage of people actually medi-tate every day. This is very interesting, because until recently these playshops were almost always held in a church set-ting. The most common reason given for not meditating is the lack of time. To that I respond: "What is the most impor-tant part of your life?" The answer is invariably "God," or "my connection with God," or my "spiritual development." But is it? If you are spending 90–100% of your time dedi-cated to "doing" and maintaining the egoic reality, is God really that important to you? Why don't we make time for God? Of course that is the subject of this book, how to put our God Self first. My suggestion is to make an "appoint-ment" with God every day. I actually ask my clients to take out their calendars or day timers and make an appointment with God in ink. (That way it is harder to erase.) Make this appointment the most important appointment of your day. You keep your lunch appointments. You show up for work on time. Why not keep your appointment with your Higher Power? It is easy to set aside time for God if your spirituality is truly the most important thing in your life. Perhaps we only pretend that our primary focus is God. I believe that our lives reveal our true focus.

Benefits

The benefits of meditation are innumerable. You clearly express to the Universe that God and your spiritual life are important to you. Equally important, you express this to yourself.

As you practice this art, you will receive exactly that which you need for your unlearning process, from ego to spirit. Because we each have journeyed through a different part of this process, meditation will be different for each of us. It is not a good idea to compare your meditations to those of others, therefore.

The Fellowship of the Heart ministerial training program includes daily writing in a journal. One of our trainees, Dawn, writes about her daily meditations which are incredible: she sees light and much more; she sees the face of Christ; angels visit her on many occasions. I began comparing my meditations to hers, questioning why I wasn't seeing what she was. Mind you, I have been meditating for about thirteen years. But comparison is never a healthy idea. Look at what we are comparing: one's perception versus another's. This will always bring up a feeling of inequity. I will feel either inferior or superior.

I visited a church in Charlottesville, VA. soon after I began comparing my meditation to Dawn's. One afternoon I talked to someone about his meditation. He mentioned that at this particular time he feels a wonderful sense of expansion while meditating; he feels as big as the room and beyond. As we were talking, I remembered when I felt that way during meditation, and that I now feel that way for 80% of my day. My *life* now feels like I used to feel while meditating. In a sense, my life has become a meditation. The important thing to remember is that whatever you feel while meditating is perfect for you at the time, and that this will change as you continue your practice. If you have played a musical instrument, or been involved in a particular sport, you know that it takes time to perfect your skill. The same is true of meditation. The practice is worth it, because whatever it is that you are feeling, and wherever you are in the process, you are receiving benefits without even being aware of them.

It may assist you to know that I find it more difficult to focus my attention on what I don't want than to focus on what I do want. As you may have noticed, I refer to meditation as a feeling, rather than a way of thinking (or not thinking). I do not try to still my mind or my thoughts when I meditate because that puts my focus on the very thing I wish to stop doing. I put my awareness on feeling, and I don't necessarily label what I want to feel. My purpose is to feel the peace of God, but labeling that seems to limit myself in some way.

It is really challenging to articulate this, because there are no words once you are in the state of expanded feeling. I can only share my process, and that may or may not assist you. Meditation has become a feeling of connection, a feeling of expanded awareness. Sometimes this includes the awareness of the body, and other times it does not. We receive many answers from this expanded state. With the background noise gone, we can see and hear solutions, feel unlimited support, and leave aside the world and its seeming insanity. Meditation is revitalizing. It charges our batteries; heals the body, the mind, and the emotions. When I come to this place of stillness, answers to all sorts of life's situations come to my awareness. Remember, you are tapping into the energy of creation. We are most connected to our Source, and thus our creative abilities, in meditation. Meditation is the best use of time that I know. Your life eventually becomes a meditation, and you find that you never need to leave this state of heightened awareness.

Meditation takes practice and patience, and it will pay off for you. It is time for me to practice that which I teach. Won't you join me?

Exercises

1. If you practice daily meditation, please congratulate yourself!

2. If you are not as yet practicing meditation on a daily basis, permit yourself to set aside a specific amount of time each day, preferably at the same time each day, to meditate. You might begin with 10–15 minutes in the morning. Eventually expand this time to 20–30 minutes.

3. Notice the impact that this practice has on your life. If you find yourself resisting this time commitment, ask yourself what is more important. Be amused by the answers that your ego gives you.

10

Be Free

"Be Free"

All my life I've always wondered who I am.
All these years I've tried to truly understand.
Is there something more that I can't hear or see?
Is there some great secret to reveal the key?

Be Free, Free as the wind. Be Free to fly like an eagle.
Be Free to bloom like a rose.
Be Free and then you will know.

And then one day the answer came quite clearly.
It told of truths that long to be set free.
So if you care to listen, what it had to say.
Is you and I are simply meant to Be.

Be Free, Free as the wind. Be Free to fly like an eagle
Be Free to bloom like a rose.
Be Free and then you will know.
"Light of the World"[1]

A s I've discussed, I have been traveling throughout the United States and abroad for the past several years visiting different ministries as a guest speaker, singer, intuitive counselor, and playshop facilitator. When I first began this traveling ministry, I wrote a song, a talk, and a workshop entitled "Be Free." For many years I had searched for the freedom that I inherently know I AM. I realize today that my search for freedom always entailed looking outside myself for someone or something that could give this freedom to me. It reminds me of the story of the man who sought the golden egg. He searched throughout the world for many years, finally, upon returning home, he found it in his own back yard.

I know now that I always had the freedom; I was simply unwilling to feel it. The following talk developed from my search for freedom, and I would like to share it with you. To this day I give this talk when I go to a church for the first time. I have asked myself many times if I should move on to a new talk for my first visit. The answer is no—give the "Be Free" talk.

Ask yourself "What do I think I need to have more freedom in my life?" Close your eyes right now and ask yourself that question. Come up with three answers. When I ask this question at the beginning of this talk I hear a variety of answers: more time, more money (I almost always get that one), forgiveness, inner peace, less judgment, a new job, letting go of expectations. If you look at these answers, you will see that several are things that we seek outside ourselves: money, time, job, while the others are attitudes that we learn to develop. These latter attitudes are the true keys to freedom.

When I wrote this talk other ideas came to mind concerning freedom. Jesus said "The truth shall set you free." But in this third-dimensional plane the truth feels very slippery to me. Just what is the truth? As I mentioned, I grew up Catholic and the "truth" I was taught in school was quite different than the truth that I choose to believe now. Although it never made any sense to me, I was taught that God is very fear-inspiring and judgmental. Today, on the other hand, I believe that God is love, joy, and peace, and that God doesn't judge—we do. So our truths change. Perhaps Truth with a capital "T" sets us free, but how many of us really know "Truth?" As I talk with different people of different faiths, I find that we have different ideas of truths; what is truth for one may not be truth for another. That doesn't make one person's truth right and the other's wrong, but they are different. Accepting these differences is one fundamental key to freedom.

Another freedom idea came to me from a book entitled *A New Pair of Glasses* by Chuck C. In it he says: *"Freedom is to not want anything at any time for yourself. This is total freedom."*[2]

Wow! At the time I read this. I felt as though I had been hit between the eyes. That sounded like freedom to me, to be free of wants and attachments. But then I thought of the many clients that I have who are not in touch with their desires, who don't know what they want in life, and who never have. They have lived their lives trying to please others, meeting others' needs, desires and expectations. Perhaps it is necessary to know what our desires are, and honor them, before we can release them.

I thought of other keys to freedom—self-discipline, courage, releasing expectations, but I sought something universal, an idea that would fit no matter your background, personality, emotional makeup, or status.

Acceptance of your life as it is now

Early in my search for freedom I attended several weekend seminars with Arnold Patent. One of his most prominent themes was "Being at peace with your life just the way it is." That is such a simple, and yet profound, idea. Being at peace with all aspects of your life, right now, just the way you are—

that would provide a tremendous sense of freedom. I wouldn't be in resistance; I wouldn't feel compelled to change or fix the externals in my life. I can choose peace now, without waiting for my or anyone else's life to change for the better. As I pondered this idea, I realized it fit my criteria. It is universal: we can practice this idea regardless of the circumstances in our lives. Choose to be at peace with all aspects of your life just the way they are: your husband, wife, or significant other; the lack of a significant other; your parents; your children; your body; your health; your bank balance; your job or lack of one; your environment; your President; your minister; your church; your present image of yourself. All of them—choose to be at peace with all of them. I would definitely feel free if I chose that.

It is important to note as well that this is not just an intellectual exercise. We need to *feel* this peace in our body for it to work. It is a wonderful idea, and it sounds as though it should work, but how do I do that?

A three step process

When I resist whatever is going on in my life, I follow a three-step process that allows me to find peace in almost any situation. The steps are: (1) feeling my feelings; (2) letting go of judgment; and (3) forgiveness.

1. FEELING MY FEELINGS

The first step in making peace with all aspects of our lives is to allow ourselves to feel our feelings. For many of us, feeling our feelings as children was not looked upon with favor, because many of our parents were not in touch with their feelings. We believed that some feelings were good—joy, hope, love, happiness, and other feelings were bad—anger, feeling hurt, jealousy, and most of all, pain. We were encouraged to feel good feelings and not feel bad feelings. Many of us received mixed messages about feelings. Sometimes it was okay to feel, while other times it was not. Sometimes we were comforted for feeling a particular feeling, and the following week we were punished for feeling the same feeling.

My ex-husband once told me a story about when he was a little boy. His older sister would tell the truth about whatever she did. She also was very good at expressing what she thought and how she felt. She usually was rewarded for sharing her thoughts and feelings, but he learned that she was only rewarded when their parents approved of her actions or beliefs. When she gave opinions that did not agree with those of their parents, she was reprimanded or corrected. It also became apparent that she could be punished when she told the truth about something that she had done that did not meet with their parents' approval. Jeff concluded that telling the truth was not always a good idea, because it might get him into trouble. He also decided that letting others know what he felt or thought could be equally dangerous, so he decided at the ripe old age of four not to let anyone know what he thought or felt. He closed down. We were both in our early twenties when I married him, and he still believed that, which caused a lot of problems for us in our relationship.

Many of us learned that it was best, or at least safest, not to feel too much, and to hide our feelings from our parents. Eventually this resulted in our hiding some feelings from ourselves, and being ashamed for the "bad" feelings that we sometimes felt. It is obvious that *many* of us received the same message, when we look at the number of people in 12-step recovery programs. In an attempt to numb ourselves, we began to abuse drugs and alcohol; we adopted other addictive behavior patterns to cover up feelings. This too we learned from our parents, and their parents, going back generations of people hiding from their feelings.

Today we are starting to allow ourselves to feel, which is a great step forward in our remembering process. Paul Tuttle, author of *You are the Answer*, once said "We are not going to think our way into Heaven, we are going to feel it." We are feeling beings, and the very act of giving ourselves permission to feel our feelings is a powerful step toward healing our minds. Day after day I hear people who are allowing themselves to feel, whatever might be the label for the feeling. It is better to feel *something* than not to feel anything at all. We need to permit ourselves to feel, and we should not judge our feelings.

I am not my feelings; I am only experiencing them

When we consider feelings from this point of view, we are no longer imprisoned by them, or by the lack of them. We can permit ourselves to feel without judgment or fear of condemnation. Now, when I have a feeling, I **embrace** it allowing me to move through it quickly. When I resist or judge the feeling, it imprisons me or it rises to the surface at some inopportune moment.

Arnold Patent teaches a technique that never fails when I use it. He instructs us to (1) feel the feeling; (2) send love to the feeling; and (3) send love to yourself for having the feeling. I have changed it a bit for my own purposes, replacing "send love to" in the second step with "embrace." It is much easier for me to embrace my anger than to send love to it. In step three, I find it quite easy to send love to myself for being a feeling person, but sometimes I find it difficult to send love to myself for having a specific feeling.

This three-step process transforms the feeling, instantaneously in many situations. I remember once when an acquaintance wanted me to provide her with information regarding a legal dispute. I did not have any knowledge that would assist her, but she pursued me relentlessly. She even harassed my mother. Finally I relented and offered to talk with her for an hour. She could ask me anything, and I would answer truthfully. To be honest, I resisted this, judging it to be an absolute waste of time. This resistance and judgment caused me pain during the entire conversation. Looking back on it, I can view it as quite funny. At the time, however, I was not amused. Afterwards, she agreed that I did not have any information that would further her case. I felt used and angry, but I really felt righteous; after all, I was right and I knew it! (I hope you don't relate!)

Seconds after hanging up the phone, it rang again. It was my friend, Peter. We talked about the prior conversation, and soon he told me, "Feel the feeling; embrace the feeling; send love to yourself for having the feeling." The feelings of anger and righteousness immediately dissolved. I felt clean, calm, and grateful for Peter's timely phone call.

The process really works. The key is to remember to do it. One way to acquire this new habit is to practice the three steps when we experience a feeling that we enjoy, rather than using the technique only when we "need" it. Another way to practice this using different words is to: (1) feel the feeling, (2) accept the feeling and the situation, (3) give the feeling and the situation to your Higher Power.

2. LETTING GO OF JUDGMENTS

We live in a world defined by judgments. People continually ask how they can live without judging. We are quite capable of observing without judging—the key is to notice whether things have a charge on them. Do people and situations push your buttons? If they do, you are judging rather than observing. An ancient Chinese philosopher said that complete freedom and happiness comes from having no preferences. Imagine yourself with no preferences. You would not care if you ate brown rice or steak; either would be fine both for your body and the planet. You would not prefer one style of clothes over another, one friend over another, one type of food, religion, book, TV program, political leader, and so on. In other words, you would not feel imprisoned by opinions, choices, and, perhaps most importantly, belief systems. How would that feel?

Whenever we judge, we fix in place whatever we judge, exactly as we judge it to be. We seal it in cement. If you want someone to stay exactly as they appear, just judge them, and they will. We believe a thing to be true when we judge, so that is how it becomes. Only when we release our judgments can we allow ourselves and others to change.

A wonderful *Star Trek* episode called the "The Empath" took place deep within a planet where beings with tall, slender bodies and very large heads lived. These beings captured Mr. Spock and Captain Kirk and encased them in energy fields. Kirk tried to escape by pushing against the energy field, but the more he resisted the stronger it became. Spock suggested that Kirk stop adding his energy to the force field (which is what we do whenever we judge). Kirk stopped, the force field dissipated immediately, and Kirk walked right through.

Similarly, when we release the judgment we hold about something or someone, that which we judged will become different in our perception. We release it from its imprisonment. Eventually, when we stop judging, we will not see anything to judge. We are much more compassionate when we refrain from judgment, and we are much happier.

I have proven this to myself in my counseling work. Whenever I have judged a person, which happens when I see the "reality" of a person's problems and focus on his/her personality rather than Divinity, they stop making progress; I perceive them to be stuck right where I judged them to be. I have only done this a few times in the many years I have been counseling, but each time the outcome is the same: my judgment (my perception) is reflected back to me.

Remember, everyone and everything in our lives acts in some way as a mirror for us. Who is it that you judge whenever you judge? Yourself. The *only* person that you can judge is yourself; you cannot judge another. Judgment is really a form of projection—I project onto you whatever I do not like, or have not come to terms with, about myself. I choose not to identify it in myself, so I must project it onto you. (Please refer back to the discussion of guilt in Chapter One.) This game keeps us very busy, putting our focus and attention outside of ourselves so that we do not work on our own destructive patterns. Instead, we try to "fix" the outside world. But since the outside world only reflects our beliefs about ourselves, the world out there will never be "fixed" until we love and accept ourselves.

An old American Indian saying states: "Never judge another unless you have walked at least one mile in his moccasins." I have no idea what is best for you. I am not living your life; I am living mine. How can I know what choices you should make, or what behavior is healthy or unhealthy for you? My path is mine and your path is yours, and I must be willing to follow my path and not try to follow yours, and I must not leave my path because you think you know what is best for me. This is co-dependency—living other people's lives instead of living our own. There is a wonderful joke I heard recently: "Have you heard the new definition of a co-dependent? It is someone who as they are dying sees **someone else's** life flash before their eyes."

Each of us has a unique path that is correct for us. For me to judge your path is to pretend that I know what is for your highest and best good. Only YOU know what that is; no one else. We can release the judgments that we have on each other when we realize this.

I believe that each act that occurs from the most heroic to the most horrific, is expressed through the Divine in each of us. God is working through everyone on this planet, from Mother Theresa to Saddam Hussein to President Clinton. We become confused when we judge Mother Theresa's actions to be good or right, and Hussein's actions to be bad or wrong. When we embrace ALL persons as children of God—when we embrace our oneness—we will stop judging. **And when we stop judging, much of the behavior that we see will stop.** The world is meaningless until we give it meaning; there is nothing out there except our perception of ourselves. Since the only person, thing, or circumstance out there is a reflection of yourself, the only person, thing, or circumstance that you judge is yourself.

The world as an amusement park

My life is Divinely guided. I believe that my true Self chooses the events in my life purposefully so that I remember the truth of who and what I really am. Each and every event in my life is a wake-up call, an opportunity for me to wake up to the truth of my Beingness. My true Self (some call this the Higher Self) knows what is best for me. It also knows that I am never in any danger. Because it sees the whole picture, it does not lose itself in the details of my life.

Look at the world as though it were a giant amusement park, a gigantic Disney World. Let us pretend that before we came to this earth we were home with each other and our Creator, safe and secure. At some point we decide that it is time for a vacation. We visit our nearest tourist office and choose a trip to Planet Earth. We will need an earth suit for our journey: a body of our choosing. It doesn't matter if it is large, small, tall, white, red, black, pretty, or plain. After all, it is just for this vacation. We also purchase a book of tickets that entitle us to every experience that we have in this lifetime.

These tickets are just like those that you would get at an amusement park, your ticket to experience any ride that you want. What is the favorite ride at an amusement park? The roller coaster. The favorite ride is the most thrilling, most dangerous, and scariest ride at the park. Why do you think you choose to have thrilling, scary, and dramatic events in your everyday life? I think that we like to be scared to death at some level. Many of us choose to live on the edge of that fear for most of our lives. Our tickets therefore include such experiences as our careers, our relationships, and our illnesses. Some have chosen AIDS as a ticket; others cancer or heart disease. Some have chosen only one partner, others several. Once we understand that each experience is a ticket that we chose, we also can choose to exchange some of the tickets and get new ones.

For many years I felt as though I was living in the amusement park from *Westworld*, an old movie with Yul Brenner where the park goes haywire and the once-friendly and co-operative robots become life-threatening. Since then I have traveled to a different amusement park, more like Disney World, and I choose to see each event as a ride that I can exit anytime. Once in a while, a roller coaster may stop and invite me on, but most of the time I choose the ride of peace or joy. I don't have to take my life so seriously. It isn't a big deal; it is just an amusing ride in a delightful amusement park.

This concept really helps me not to judge. Everyone is riding whatever ride they want. If it is just a ride, then there is nothing to fear and very little to take seriously. It is a very freeing concept.

3. FORGIVENESS

When I practice the concepts discussed above, it becomes incredibly easy to forgive. And the very desire to forgive allows me to let go of judgments. Sometimes forgiveness doesn't seem so easy, but I still practice these concepts. Forgiveness is to me almost magical. It changes my perception of my past. I would like to share an interesting roller coaster ride that helped me to understand the real power of forgiveness.

Several years ago I "fell in love." Have you ever asked yourself where you "fall to" when you "fall in love?" I *really* fell hard. This man was my "knight in shining armor." Why do we choose partners who wear armor? That makes them pretty unavailable doesn't it? Of course, that brings up another question: why do some of us choose "sleeping beauties"? A comatose partner isn't much of a joy to be with either. This guy was my prince, and his steed was a white Toyota 4-Runner. Believe it or not, he lived in the town of "Rescue," in California, where he had a gorgeous home. He invited me to live with him happily for ever after. Never mind the red flags that he was only six months out of a 25-year marriage and that he had four daughters that he was just getting to know— I was In Love, and love is blind.

We went on a month long trip right before I was to move in. I was just beginning my touring career, and I was teaching the process of making peace with your life just the way it is. You can imagine how easy this was for me. I had my knight and I was moving to Rescue—all was right with my world.

Halfway into the trip, my prince informed me that he did not want me to move in with him, and that he wanted me to go back home when we returned to Rescue. My first reaction was denial: "He doesn't mean it. If I'm just a little different, or better, he'll change his mind." The rest of the trip became a different kind of a roller coaster ride for me, because I chose to see the ride as scary, rather than thrilling. Mind you, it really was the same roller coaster. When we returned home, he put my suitcases at the door of my car. I finally realized that he was not kidding.

I felt an intense pain that I did not want to feel. I asked why we choose to feel pain, and I heard this answer: "When we have chosen to close our hearts, pain can be used to "crack" them open again. We choose pain to open our hearts." My heart sure felt cracked, so I asked it to open. I decided that it might be a great idea to practice the three steps that I had been teaching. We teach that which we most need to learn, and this certainly applied to me at this moment. I felt my feelings. I embraced my feelings, and by embracing the pain, it changed. Instead of resisting the pain and creating a "force field" around it, I chose to feel it fully. This allowed me to work through the pain rather quickly, in weeks rather than months.

My next step was to let go of judgments. I really didn't have a lot of judgments on my prince from Rescue at the time. The judgments I needed to release were the ones I had placed upon myself: why did I create this reality? What was wrong with me? At the same time I forgave myself and I forgave him. As I continued to forgive, I realized that there was someone else I needed to forgive: my father. I recognized that I had put the face of my father on every man with whom I had had a relationship, looking to them to heal my childhood wounds and provide the love that I did not feel from my dad. So I forgave my father. I thought that I had already forgiven my father, but it was obvious that I was not finished. So I began the wondrous process of forgiveness again. I did every exercise I know: I wrote 7 times 70* "I forgive you, dad." I brought him into my meditations and forgave. I invited my inner child into the meditations and asked her to forgive.

Several months later I had one of the most powerful experiences of my life. One afternoon, as I sat down to meditate, I was brought back to the time when I was eight months old. I was being held by someone, and as I looked into his eyes, I saw the eyes of absolute, unconditional love. It was my dad. Then I was five years old, walking hand in hand with my dad in San Francisco's Golden Gate Park. Again, I looked up into his eyes and saw absolute, unconditional love. It was a

---

* Write 70 times per day for 7 days in a row, "I forgive _____
(person you are forgiving) for _____
(whatever you wish to forgive them for).

profound experience. I realized that my dad was incapable of anything other than unconditional love. What makes this so powerful is that as a child, I was very afraid of my father. Prior to this experience, I had memories of my dad trying to kill my mother, my brother and myself, in addition to many other terrifying situations. I remember very clearly believing the devil lived in our house, in the body of my father.

Understanding at a deep level that my dad could only be a giver of love meant that my forgiveness process with him was complete. I now have a different memory of my childhood. When I look back on events that seemed chaotic and frightening, I see my father asking for help and love, or I remember an entirely different scene. My perception of my father and my childhood has changed, and with it my past. We can change our past with forgiveness. After all, the past is only our *perception* of what we remember it to be; when we change our perception, we change our past. I am no longer a victim of my past, or believe that I did not receive love from my dad.

This story has a very happy ending. The prince and I parted company, and I met another wonderful man upon whom I did not put the face of my dad. We married on Christmas Eve of 1992, and we have a healthy, happy, and joy-filled relationship. I am free in this relationship to be me, and do whatever it is that I am guided to do. Whenever I think that I want something different in my life, I practice the three steps: (1) I feel my feelings; (2) I let go of any judgments I have about the person or situation; and (3) I forgive.

There is a fourth step that may or may not be appropriate for you: action. After forgiveness, you may feel that there is some action that you wish to take. In the above example, I chose to leave the relationship. After forgiving, I saw that the relationship was not for my highest and best good. Naturally, if it was not for mine, it was not for his either. The best action was to move on. But actions chosen before taking the three steps are sometimes based upon something other than clarity, and can be taken out of fear or resentment. As previously mentioned, decisions made from a state of fear usually need to be made again. Decisions made from a state of resentment have a strong underlying motive of punishment or vengeance. It was clear to me what action I needed to take after I had completed the three steps. I could not decide on an action before then. I wait before I take action until I feel a sense of peace about myself and the situation, unless of course I am in physical danger. A cute rhyme helps me decide whether or not it is time to DO something: **"If in doubt; wait it out."** I am not forced to make a series of decisions that may or may not be empowering to myself or others.

11

Be Free–Meditations & Exercises

I t may be very beneficial to put the following exercises on tape for yourself. You also may purchase the book on tape, which includes these exercises. As you prepare to do the guided meditations, allow your predominant sense to guide you through the experience. For those who are visually oriented, the exercise will be very visual; for those who are kinesthetic the exercise will be felt. There are no wrong or right ways to do these exercises.

A guided journey on finding a safe place

Sit in a comfortable position and focus on your breath. Take several long slow breaths and relax your body. Imagine a golden ball of light one foot above your head sending warm, soothing light down into your head and body. As you breathe, allow your sensation of the breath to move up into your head and merge with the golden light. Allow the breath to move into your scalp area and feel your scalp relaxing. Next, move your awareness into your face, your cheek muscles, your mouth and tongue, and allow them to relax. Allow the back of your neck to relax. Your whole head is relaxed. Breathe into your throat and let it relax. Allow your chest and upper arms to relax. Move the breath down your arms and hands and let them relax. Breathe into your upper back, and let the

breath flow down your spine, relaxing your entire back. Let
the internal organs and muscles relax. Let your stomach drop
to where it belongs. Allow your hips and buttocks to feel
relaxed. Allow this relaxation to move down into your thighs
and knees and finally your feet. Feel your entire body relaxed and at peace. Continue to breathe long, slow, deep
breaths.

Imagine yourself on a path. It is a beautiful path. There
may be flowers along the side of the path, or small bushes or
perhaps some tall trees. The sky is blue, with some white
puffy clouds. You might hear birds singing, or a gentle wind
in the trees. It is a lovely day, and you are ready to be at
peace with yourself and your life, just the way it is.

You see a small foot bridge in the distance, and you feel
anticipation and a readiness to cross over as you approach
it. You know that something wonderful is on the other side
of this bridge. But you feel a little discomfort as you approach
the bridge. It could be a heaviness, especially around your
neck and on your upper back. You realize that you are carrying a backpack filled with the stuff of your life: your beliefs,
worries, hopes, dreams, and fears. Take off the backpack before you cross the bridge. Very gently, take the shoulder straps
off and lower the pack to the ground. Free yourself of its
heaviness and of the burdens that you carry. Feel the freedom that is yours when you remove this pack—the light-
ness, the ease and grace that is naturally yours. If you want,
you can pick it up later when you cross back over the bridge,
but for now leave the backpack on the ground.

Now cross over the bridge. On the other side of this bridge
is a beautiful space. It is your space, safe, secure, and free
from outside influences. No one can come into this space
unless you request. This is your sacred place to come to whenever you choose. If you already have a sacred place, it may
be the same space, or it may be a new space that you create
for this time. It is yours, and you can create it in any way you
like: at the ocean, in a wondrous garden, in a room some-

where, or it may be a combination of several places. Wherever it is, it is yours to create just as you want.

After you have spent some time exploring your space, thank yourself for creating such a magnificent place for yourself and come gently back over the bridge. For now, leave the backpack on the ground. Walk back up the path. As you do, bring your conscious awareness back to the room in which you are sitting. Gently open your eyes when you are ready.

An exercise in letting go of judgment

Repeat this relaxation exercise and travel to your sacred space. Before you cross the bridge, notice the condition of your backpack. If you had picked it up before, put it down again before crossing over the bridge.

Now that you are once again in your safe place, spend a little time here, feeling the safety, seeing the beauty and allowing yourself to feel the peace of this place…

From this sense of peace and safety, allow yourself to get in touch with a relationship, perhaps with your parents, or situation in your life where you hold judgment, or where you seem to feel stuck. Allow yourself to get in touch with one person, and simply allow that person to enter your conscious awareness.

Ask this person to come into your sacred place. Remember, this is your place, and no one can enter without your permission. This is a totally safe place for you at all times. (If you resist this person's entry, create a Plexiglas wall at the edge of your space and invite the person to come that far. This will provide an additional feeling of security).

Tell this person whatever you would like to say, perhaps your judgment, perhaps an undelivered communication. Do not judge what you wish to say. Remember, this is an exercise in letting go of our judgments, and one way to do that is to release them through words. Be as clear and complete as you can with your message, and allow yourself to feel whatever feelings you have as you say whatever it is that you want to say.

When you feel complete, allow the person to respond as completely as he or she can. (This part of the exercise is extremely powerful, and can bring clarity and completion). When he/she is complete, thank him/her for coming into your space and ask the person to leave. Choose to be at peace once more. When you are ready, cross over the bridge. As you walk up the path, come back into complete awareness of your body and where you are in the present moment.

(Note: In the "Be Free" playshop, we next split into pairs. We do the same exercise again, with our partner acting as proxy for the person that you brought into your sacred place. The proxy listens without reply to your communication, until you have said all that you said in the meditation. This is not a third-party exercise. If you brought in your mother, you treat the proxy as if your mother was sitting there, call the proxy "Mom" and say word for word what you said in the meditation. When you are finished, the proxy responds in the role of the person you invited. If you brought in your mother, the proxy would pretend to be your mother and respond to your delivered communication. What the proxy says in response may be different than what you heard in the meditation, which can give you even greater clarity and completion. This is a very powerful exercise; it would be most beneficial if you feel drawn to do this. Both you and the proxy complete the above exercises, taking turns being one another's proxies.)

An exercise in forgiveness

Relax your body as in the above exercise and enter your sacred space. Check the condition of your backpack before you cross over the bridge. Please take it off again, if you need to.

As you become aware of your safe place again, notice that there is a child here. This child is your inner child, the child that lives inside of you. Invite the child to come closer. As he/she does, take a close look at yourself as this child. How old are you? What are you wearing? How do you feel as this child? Are you happy, sad, secure, fearful? Do you have a connection with this child? Does the child know who you are? Does he or she trust you? How do you feel about this child? Invite the child closer, and take the child to where the two of you can sit. Invite the child to sit on your lap. If the child is unwilling to do this, have the child sit next to you. Notice how all of this feels.

Ask the child to forgive you for anything that you have done, or failed to do, that may have hurt him/her, whether through neglect or by consciously not meeting his/her needs. Ask for forgiveness and be willing to accept it. Talk with your child awhile and ask him/her what it is that she/he needs from you at this time. If it feels appropriate, promise that you will give this to your child. Hold your child and tell him/her that you love him/her and that you will always be there for him/her. Tell the child that he/she is a part of you, and that you intend to nourish and protect him/her from now on. Allow your child to respond. Do not judge any part of this process, either by judging yourself or your child. Just let the process flow.

When you and your child feel safe with one another, or at least have established a rapport, decide with your child who you will now invite into your space to forgive. I suggest that you start with someone who is easy to forgive; it is not necessary for us to pick the most challenging person in our lives to forgive first. Do not try to analyze who this should be. The person's face will simply come up in your awareness. (Please note that at some point this may be yourself. The person also may be in or out of body, since you can very easily do these exercises with people who have died.)

Once you know who you are both going to forgive, invite this person into your sacred space. Allow him/her to sit with you and your child. Decide with your child which of you will speak first, and give yourself the gift of this time together. Each of you, one at a time, say whatever it is that you need to say. Be as complete as possible in your communication, and feel your feelings as fully as you can when you deliver your message. When both you and the child have forgiven this person to the best of your ability, allow the person to respond. Allow this person to be as complete as possible, without any expectation on your part. When the person has finished, thank him/her for coming in to share with you and invite him/her to leave.

Embrace and thank the child for the wonderful job that he/she just did. Tell the child once more that you love him/her, and that you will see him/her again soon. Allow the child to play in your sacred space, or place the child gently next to your heart and invite him/her in so that you can be with your child at all times. Look around at your sacred place, feel it fully, and thank yourself for creating it. Cross back over the footbridge and decide what you want to do with your backpack. Start back up the path and come into full conscious awareness of yourself in present time.

(As in the previous exercise, in the workshop we pair off again with a different partner and do this exercise in the same manner as before.)

12

Forgiveness: A Key to Abundance

" Forgiveness is the great need of this world, but that is because it is a world of illusions. Those who forgive are thus releasing themselves from illusions, while those who withhold forgiveness are binding themselves to them. As you condemn only yourself, so do you forgive only yourself." [1]

" You who want peace can find it only by complete forgiveness... While lack does not exist in the creation of God, it is very apparent in what you have made." [2]

—A Course in Miracles

W e touched on the concept of forgiveness in Chapter Ten, and since its benefits are beyond anything
else I know let us explore it further.

Forgiveness is a key to happiness, prosperity, health, peace,
abundance, and especially relationships. You might say that
forgiveness is the key to freedom. You are free when you are in a
forgiving place. If you are in an unforgiving place, on the
other hand you will feel blocked. This feeling will manifest
itself as lack and limitation in one of the above areas.

Forgiveness is one of the greatest gifts that you can give to
yourself and to others. It always works, and I use it a lot. I
know that forgiveness is part of our ego belief system, but
forgiveness truly empowers us, and frequently assists us in
moving beyond our judgments. If my life is not flowing in
any area, including health, I know that I should practice forgiveness, for forgiveness truly can be a key to abundance in
every single area of life.

Remember the old round:

"Row, row, row your boat, gently down the stream.
Merrily, merrily, merrily, merrily, life is but a dream."

That is how life can feel when you practice forgiveness.
No matter the situation, no matter how much it feels like
you are paddling upstream, when you open yourself to forgiveness, your boat (your life) turns around and travels gently down the stream.

Failure to forgive creates lack and limitation

You withhold when you are unwilling to forgive—you are
not willing to give forgiveness. When you are unwilling to
give, you will usually experience a lack or limitation in your
life, for the universe reflects what you are doing. You are not
allowing the energy of the Universe to flow through you,

and as a result you will *experience* the Universe withholding from you, as limitations in money, work, relationship, health, happiness, whatever. In short, you will experience lack. In reality, though, the Universe is not withholding from you. It can't! The Universe is the natural expression of abundance. You only FEEL a lack because you are withholding from yourself, and therefore blocking the natural flow of the Universe. The escape from this dilemma is to forgive.

> *" Forgiveness thus undoes what fear has produced, returning the mind to the awareness of God. For this reason, forgiveness can truly be called salvation. It is the means by which illusions disappear."*[3]
>
> **—A Course in Miracles**

We usually have anger when we are unwilling to forgive, and we often use it in an attempt to make someone feel guilty. When we are invested in feeling angry, we are equally invested in playing the role of victim. One wouldn't invest any energy in anger unless one felt victimized. The December 7, 1993 *Washington Post* featured a long article about a former Catholic priest who was convicted of over 28 counts of sexual child abuse. The "victims," who are now adults in their thirties and forties, blamed the priest for **all** of their problems—failed marriages, alcoholism, drug abuse, job failures. They were furious and wanted revenge, saying things like, "No punishment would be too extreme," "He should be castrated," and "Life imprisonment would not be enough."

These people in their anger clearly are attempting to make this man feel guilty. I would venture to say that it is more their lack of forgiveness rather than the actual abuse that has caused the problems in their lives. I am not saying that the abuse did not have an effect. I **am** saying that if the child had been taught forgiveness at the time, and if the parents had been willing to forgive as well, the child might have dealt with the situation very differently. Instead, the horror, outrage, denial and other reactions had an even greater impact on these children. This priest obviously had a sexual addiction, an illness that needed to be treated. But, again, his illness/addiction was a cry for love.

What if all acts are either demonstrations of or cries for love? Logically speaking, we were created by Love and thus must be an extension of this Love. All acts, no matter how they appear, therefore must have something to do with Love. When we understand this, we can respond with love, rather than hate, even to violent acts. In this situation, for example, the priest was crying for love. We may judge his act to be wrong, abusive, and extremely inappropriate, but it was still a cry for love. The anger we now observe in his "victims" also is a cry for love. If these children and their parents had been able to forgive, they now would experience love, because forgiveness is simply another aspect of love. They did not extend love or forgiveness, however, and so do not feel love. When we do not feel love, we will cry out for it. This reaction often looks like anger, judgment, and attack, which is exactly what these people are doing to this priest.

The way to end the cycle is to forgive. It takes a lot of courage to be the first to begin the process. I hope that soon we will find ourselves in a society that no longer feels the need for punishment. As we learn to recognize cries for love, responding to them as such, we will learn to ask for love in less violent ways.

An excellent example of what I am talking about appears in the Winter 1995 issue of *Miracles Magazine* at page seven. An article entitled "Hartford pastor officiates at wedding of son's killer" tells the story of the Rev. Walter H. Everett of Bridgeport, Connecticut, whose son, Scott, was fatally shot by 24 year old Michael Carlucci. When he was told that

Carlucci would spend five years in prison as a result of a plea bargain agreement, Everett was angry. He didn't feel like it was enough. On the one year anniversary of Scott's death, however, Everett wrote Carlucci in prison to offer forgiveness. The two became close friends, and Everett officiated at Carlucci's wedding. At the ceremony Everett said: "'I'm sorry' and 'I forgive you' are the two key words in any relationship." Reading from the Bible he continued: "Love is patient and kind. Love bears all things, believes all things, hopes all things, endures all things." Carlucci credited Everett's unconditional love with helping him redeem his life since the fatal shooting.

Forgiveness in relationships

It is imperative that we practice forgiveness in our more intimate relationships. We must be willing to forgive those we live with on a daily basis. Sometimes this may be more challenging than forgiving someone who we do not know. I remember a counseling session that I gave to a woman many years ago. She shared that she could not forgive her husband and had closed her heart to him, although she had allowed it to remain open to everyone else.

I told her that even though I did not want to disagree, if she closed her heart to one person, she closed it to everyone. John Gray in his book *What Your Mother Couldn't Tell You & Your Father Didn't Know,* addresses the importance of forgiveness in our close personal relationships:

> *" To fully open our hearts to each other and enjoy a lifetime of love, the most important skill of all is forgiveness. Forgiving your partner for their mistakes not only frees*

> *you to love again but allows you to*
> *forgive yourself for not being*
> *perfect.*
>
> *" When we don't forgive in one*
> *relationship, our love is, to various*
> *degrees, restricted in all our life*
> *relationships.*
>
> *" We can still love others, but not as*
> *much. When a heart is blocked in*
> *one relationship, it beats more*
> *weakly in them all."* [4]

When you close your heart to one person, it affects every relationship that you have, including with God and with yourself.

Forgiveness of ourselves

It is as important to forgive ourselves as it is to forgive others. As we discussed earlier, we stop blaming others and turn that blame upon ourselves during the process of remembering who we are. While reading the book *Peace Pilgrim* I realized that forgiving others and not ourselves is Spiritual arrogance. Peace places a strong emphasis on the importance of forgiving ourselves in her discussion of forgiveness:

> *" During the preparation period I*
> *wasn't fully identifying with the*
> *real me, I was just learning. I was*
> *very forgiving toward others, that*

*was no problem, but I was very
unforgiving toward myself. If I did
something that wasn't the highest,
I would say to myself, 'You ought
to know better.' And then one day
as I was combing my hair at the
mirror, I looked at myself and said,
'You vain thing! Why do you think
you know better when you forgive
everyone else for not knowing
better? You're not any better than
they are.'*

" *You must learn to forgive yourself
as easily as you forgive others. And
then take a further step and use all
that energy that you used in
condemning yourself for improving
yourself. After that I really started
to get somewhere—because there's
only one person you can change
and that's yourself. After you have
changed yourself, you might be able
to inspire others to look for change.*

" *It took the living quite awhile to
catch up with the believing but it
finally did. And when it did, a
progress began which never ended.
As I lived up to the highest light I*

*had, higher and higher light came
to me."*[5]

A key to health

Withholding forgiveness also effects our health. The lack of
forgiveness creates tension and cellular shutdown within the
physical body. Anger becomes very destructive in the human body over time. Our emotions directly affect our bodies and the quality of our health. Dr. Bernie Siegel in *Love
Medicine and Miracles* says:

> *"Often I can suggest exactly what
> the patient's emotional troubles
> are, based on the symptoms and
> location of their disease."*[6]

Imagine anger as hot, red, and violent, like an erupting
volcano. Now imagine anger suppressed in the body over
years, or perhaps expressed as a series of continual outbursts.
What do you think that would do to the body? Every tissue,
organ, and system in our body is controlled by a complex
interaction of chemicals in the brain. Every thought that you
think, every feeling you feel, has a direct impact on these
chemicals, and therefore on your health. Over time, anger
will destroy and forgiveness will heal. This is not to say that
occasional outbursts of anger are "bad," but continual sup-
pression or expression of anger is very harmful to the body.
Anger also hides a deeper emotion—fear. I have heard this
over and over again at counseling sessions. We are never
angry for the reason we think. I have never experienced anger without eventually acknowledging the underlying fear,
and this seems to be a universally held understanding.

Bernie Siegel suggests that:

> *" To unblock the fountain of love and enter on the path of creative, spiritual growth, we must let go of our fears."*[7]

Forgiveness does this. Forgiveness wipes the slate clean, and forgiveness (unconditional love) is the greatest stimulant to our bodies' immune system. In other words, love heals and anger destroys.

Karma and the state of grace

Karma is one of the most ridiculous ego beliefs we have ever devised. In principle it is based on the law of cause and effect, loosely translated as "What goes around, comes around." The law of cause and effect says that all began with God, and we as God's children have the ability to create in God's image. Our thoughts create form, and thus the form we perceive began in our minds. We therefore need to monitor our thoughts and choose love, rather than anger, since love thoughts create one type of world and anger thoughts an entirely different type. Your world is *literally* determined by the thoughts you think. The law of cause and effect also says that you will receive whatever you give: if you give love, you will receive love: if you give time or help, you will receive time or help; this is true with judgments, anger, hatred, punishment—the Universe is very fair.

Karma seems to be on a very individual basis, however. If I do something to you in this lifetime (either bad or good), you are obligated to pay me back in this lifetime or another. Karma thus is similar to cause and effect, only individualized. We often think of it in relation to punishment, judg-

ment, and guilt. What better way to perpetuate the ego system than to make up a belief like karma? If you don't get me
back in this lifetime, you get another chance in the next one!

Remember what we experience is what we believe to be
true. So if we believe that we have to keep coming back until
we have "burned off" all of our karma, until we "get it right,"
or until we are "even," that is what we will experience. But
who determines when we "get it right" or when we are
"even?" God certainly did not devise karma or reincarnation. Karma is born of the need to punish, and fits right into
this level of three dimensional reality.

Forgiveness creates the state of grace

Grace is the state when you consciously feel connected to
God. It erases karmic debt. Forgiveness removes us from the
karmic wheel and brings us into present time in which we
are consciously connected with God. When you and I feel
this conscious connection, there is no longer the need for
punishment, because our perception comes much closer to
reality and we begin to "see" with more self-esteem and self-
love. We no longer believe that we deserve punishment. You
can still hold vestiges of an older and different belief when
you move into a new system of belief, however. Forgiveness
will help release your belief in karma (punishment) entirely,
because forgiveness creates grace.

Forgiveness = Forgetting

Among its many benefits, grace allows us to be in the present
moment. It keeps us centered in the NOW. When we forgive, we release the past, our attachment to it, and, eventually, our memories of it. Forgiveness allows us to change our
perception of the past. Our past is only what we *think* it was,
and many times this really has nothing to do with what real-

ly happened. We always interpret what is going on around us, and we perceive things from our own point of view. No two people have the same perception of the same event. Marsha Sinetar, in her book *Do What You Love the Money Will Follow* says that:

> " ...*our self view comes from our childhood, what we were taught about ourselves. Our primary care takers taught us if we were lovable, okay, capable, able to solve problems, or not okay, stupid, slow, unlovable... If I hold a low self image of myself, I am in fact judging myself and therefore in a state of non-forgiveness. Therefore I will perceive events and people through the filter of judgment and low self esteem. If I still judge my parents, I will carry that judgment over to other authority figures i.e. teachers, politicians, bosses, ministers etc.*"[8]

True forgiveness means understanding that the person that you forgive never did anything to you in the first place. If all actions are either an extension of love or a cry for love, what is there to forgive?

I recently watched an episode of *Rosanne* in which Rosanne's sister Jackie had sex with a married guy, Arnie. All of Jackie's friends were amazed that she could stoop to such a sleazy act as having sex with Arnie, of all people. Rosanne talked about this with her husband, and he said:

"Well Rosanne, if Jackie would feel the need to do such a thing, I think it was a cry for love." Rosanne replied: "More like a scream."

Exactly! Most of us weren't taught to ask for love. Many of us wouldn't have received love, even if we had asked, because our parents had not been taught either. So we did what we saw our parents and other teachers do: we acted out our pain and fear. We cried for love. When we understand that people are in pain, feel unlovable, and are crying for help, it is easy to forgive their actions. We understand that their actions were a cry for us to love them.

Recently at a playshop the topic was forgiveness. A man shared that his wife had told him, "Well, I am going to forgive you, but I'm not going to forget." That does not sound like forgiveness to me. Instead, it sounds very conditional, and it feels like resentment just waiting to happen. I can see her waiting for the next time that he does something "wrong," coming out with both barrels: "See, you did it again," or some variation on that theme.

My past changed entirely when I completed my forgiveness process with my dad. I only remember happy things, and try as I might, the more gruesome memories are not there. I have become a product of a functional, loving, happy family. Imagine the freedom that gives me. I am no longer a product of an unhappy childhood. I no longer saddle myself with the problems that come with being an adult child of an alcoholic. I am not talking about denial! By truly forgiving my parents, I truly changed my past. This has opened a new world to me. Through forgiveness, I am free to see and know the truth about all of us—that we are love, and *only* love. Everything else is smoke and mirrors, part of the illusion of our unworthiness.

When I dwell in the past, I remember it the way **I** thought it was. I often used the past to feel guilt, since it is very easy to use the past as a way to punish myself. When I project into the future, I am usually in the land of expectation or fear of the unknown. The safest and most effective place I can be is here, in the Now. In the present, I can plan for my future without expectations, and I can release the past and its guilt. Forgiveness allows me to do this with grace and ease.

Forgiveness = For Giving

Being willing to give everything I have is one of the greatest gifts I can give myself. When I am unwilling to give of myself, I stop my prosperity, because I tell myself that my supply is limited. In addition, I give myself the message that my abundance comes from *outside* of me, rather than *through* me.

A few years ago I was asked to speak at a Course in Miracles Center and do an afternoon workshop. I was told that the fee for speaking was $35, and almost laughed. I thought: "why bother; that doesn't even pay for my gas." I explained what my minimum fee was, and how I no longer wanted to give my time away. As I listened to what I was saying, I remembered my teaching: "When I am unwilling to give of myself, I stop my prosperity, because I tell myself that my supply is limited." I viewed this Center and the people there as my supply, forgetting that the Universe is my supply, and that the Universe is unlimited. I am the only person who limits my supply. I could believe that this Center is doing the same thing—limiting their supply by refusing to pay me my fee. But where does that get me? NOWHERE. This only diverts my mind from its inner work. The issue is whether I am willing to show up and give of myself. The Universe will compensate me if I am willing to give, and if I am willing to receive.

To demonstrate my point, I did in fact take the job that offered me $35. Within a few days, the person who had referred me for this engagement called to find out if I had been hired, and if the arrangements were satisfactory. I told him

We Never Left the Garden

that I had accepted their offer and when I was going to be there. He asked me what my normal fee was, and told me he was putting a check in the mail for that amount that very day. I was willing to serve and give of myself, and the Universe supported this decision. I might not have been open to the abundance if I were coming from a place of sacrifice.

The Universe also allows me to practice the principles I incorporate into my life. For instance, while writing this section I received a call from a friend who needed a ride to a 12-step meeting at noon. This provides an opportunity to practice what I teach, to give of myself, for it will take about an hour to pick him up and drop him off. Since time is unlimited, though, I am again given an opportunity to **live** these principles. Some people say that the Universe "tests" you. As I have written in other sections of this book, I don't believe that the word "test" is supportive, because we set ourselves up to pass or fail. I view this as an **opportunity**.

Serving vs. Sacrifice

Within minutes of the above conversation, another friend, Margot, called. I shared with her the synchronicity of this event, and she immediately asked "Okay, but when is it sacrifice? I have a hard time knowing the difference between serving and sacrificing. Couldn't doing something that someone else wants me to do be a sacrifice?" Margot was calling me to ask a question about a brochure that she was producing for me as a gift. I asked her if this brochure felt like a sacrifice. She said no, it was fun and she was very happy to do it. I suggested to her that her gift of her time illustrated how the abundance of the universe works. I gave my other friend my time and transportation, and at the same time Margot gave me a free brochure! (By the way, this happens to me all the time.)

I had been exhausted the previous day, and thus it could have felt like a sacrifice if my friend had called and asked for a ride that day. It is readily apparent if we are serving or sacrificing when we ask ourselves how an action feels. It also depends upon our intent, or our perception of the event. Remember, sacrifice is never justified. To sacrifice is to align with the idea of lack, because to sacrifice is to give up something, to suffer loss. This is never purposeful, because this implies that the Universe is limited. I know that there is someone else out there who can take this friend to a meeting if I am too tired, or he can take a bus or walk. There is an unlimited supply of everything, but we must be open to accepting it. This is where most of the difficulty lies.

On some level we still feel unworthy and unable to receive, and thus we close ourselves off from our abundance, by sacrificing. It's the same old pattern of punishing ourselves because of the guilt we feel from our supposed separation from our Source, God. This is quite purposeful, because we finally see how simple the whole process of our choosing pain really is. Once again, forgiveness is the key to freedom.

Living your dream

Forgiveness allows the creative force of the Universe to flow through us. If I am experiencing scarcity in any area of my life, I know I need to practice forgiveness. This brings me to the last idea in this chapter: forgiveness allows you to get in touch with and live your dream. If you are not in touch with your dream, your purpose in your life, or you are not living it, you probably need to forgive. The only reason you are not living your dream is because you do not feel that you deserve it. This results from judging yourself, which creates low self-esteem. It does not matter where you learned to judge yourself. What matters is that you stop. Forgive yourself, and you will express in the world. Forgive others, and you forgive yourself. Forgive and experience the abundance that is your natural birthright as a child of the Universe.

Exercises

1. Repeat the relaxation exercise in Chapter Eleven. Forgive all the different areas of your body: your organs, your muscles, your bones, your senses (sight, hearing, touch, taste, smell, feelings), your skin, any part of your body that you judge as having let you down. Send love to those areas.

2. Repeat the forgiveness exercise in Chapter Eleven. Go into your special place and bring in your mother, following all the steps in the exercise.

3. Repeat the above exercise with your father.

4. Repeat the above exercise with yourself.

5. Inventory where and when you find it difficult to give. What are the excuses you use? Ask yourself: what decision did I make that keeps me unwilling to give in this area of my life? Am I willing to make a different decision? Am I willing to see this differently?" If so, write how you would like to see it and feel about it, and start the practice of giving in this area.

13

Beyond Addiction

What is an "addiction?" What does it mean to be an "addict?" Webster's defines an addict and addiction as: "To devote or surrender (oneself) to something habitually or obsessively. 2: one who is addicted to a drug."

In today's society we have become aware of addiction and the many forms it can take. Numerous 12-step programs have been established to deal with these addictions: Alcoholics Anonymous, Narcotics Anonymous, Adult Children of Alcoholics, Workaholics Anonymous, Emotions Anonymous, Debtors Anonymous, Over-Eaters Anonymous, Co-Dependents Anonymous, Smokers Anonymous, Shoppers Anonymous, Sex and Love Addicts Anonymous, Gamblers Anonymous, and the list grows every month.

That means there are over one dozen *well-known*, separate, and identified addictive behaviors from which people consider themselves to be recovering. Charles L. Whitfield, M.D. in his book, *Co-dependence: Healing the Human Condition*,[1] lists over thirty-six recovery programs in the back of his book under *Resources*, and there are rumored to be over 300 different recovery programs in the United States. I have heard many people in 12-step meetings call themselves "cross-addicted," meaning that they acknowledge an addiction to more than one substance or behavior. Most people have heard of AA (Alcoholics Anonymous), but the majority do not feel that they qualify for a 12-step program. Jed Diamond in his book *Looking for Love in All the Wrong Places* writes that *"one American in 12 is addicted. Only one in 100 knows it."*[2]

Why this sudden increase in the number of recovery programs, and in the number of books on the recovery process? I believe that everyone on this planet is addicted. Anyone who considers him/herself to be human is an addict, and the sudden increase in the attendance, number, and variety of recovery programs is a recognition of this fact.

The Pattern of addiction

Addictions come in a variety of forms. But each form is only a ruse, a smoke screen that hides the underlying addiction—we are all addicted to pain. (For those of you who are currently active in a 12- step program please read on before you throw this book across the room!) Let us review for a minute the metaphor in Chapter One of the child deciding to leave home (our Source). We felt guilt at the very core of our humanness. As we discussed, this guilt arose because of our attempt to separate from God, our Source. We attempt to pay for this guilt by inflicting pain upon ourselves and each other. We have become addicted to this process, habitually surrendering to feeling separate from one another, and from our Source, and to the feeling of pain. We constantly obsess about pain. Almost every story on the evening news deals with pain: the pain of war, murder, robbery, hunger, fire, and flood. We replay the same scenarios over and over again. Guilt leads to the infliction of pain; it will never end as long as we continue to believe in our guilt. The names, dates, and characters may change, but the pattern stays the same.

I was watching a movie the other night called "The Untouchables." It took place during the years of prohibition, when alcohol was illegal in the United States. The principle adversaries were Al Capone, a gang leader and major smuggler of booze into this country and Eliott Ness, the cop who was going to "uphold the law no matter what the cost!" I was fascinated as I watched. We are doing exactly the same thing today, with the war on drugs, gang wars, and killings, with our prisons filled to capacity with marijuana and cocaine dealers. I have seen our patterns before but never with such clarity. We repeat the same patterns over and over so that we can feel separate and continue to inflict pain upon ourselves and one another. We are indeed addicted to pain and suffering.

Reincarnation as part of the pattern

Another way to look at the repetition of patterns is through the belief in reincarnation. Suppose for a moment that we actually do reincarnate and have a series of lifetimes. What a clever way to continue feeling separate from God! As soon as we leave this body, we go to a place where we await the entrance into another one. During an evening group session, I was given the amusing picture of seeing our present life as a ride on a Ferris wheel. When the ride is finished, we run as fast as we can to purchase a ticket and get in line for another ride (another incarnation) on the **same** Ferris wheel. Some people believe that there are millions of souls out there waiting to re-enter the physical experience. The practice of reincarnation reflects an obsessive need to be in a body, and therefore to experience pain. One could therefore say that we are addicted to bodies, the physical manifestation of form.

Let us assume then that we are all addicts, and that the underlying addiction is to separation and pain. How do we stop this addictive behavior? How do we release ourselves from the need to punish ourselves?

Steps in Recovery: Acknowledgment

We need to acknowledge our tendency toward addiction, and the fact that we all are addicted on some level. This may not be obvious to you. You may not be addicted to food, to drugs, to work, to relationships, or you may still be in denial about your addiction. Just acknowledge that we have very strong addictive tendencies.

All addictions deal with **denial** at some level. An obvious example of this is the behavior of an alcoholic. Many alcoholics drink without knowing they are "alcoholic." They deny to themselves and to others that they have a problem with alcohol. Alcoholics commonly blame their problems on everyone else. The statement "If it weren't for you, I wouldn't drink" is well known to people who have lived with alcoholics. (This is also a perfect example of projection.) Many alcoholics continue to drink even after they become aware of their drinking problem, because they still deny that they need to stop.

Almost everyone denies their addiction to pain and their addiction to feeling separate from God. Many of us say "I want to be home, I want to be consciously with God, to know who I AM." The truth is we would experience conscious connection with God if we would commit to it. Since we are whole, perfect, and an extension of our Source what could be easier than to feel that which we already ARE? Instead we deny that we are addicted to our separation from our Source. But, as the metaphor in Chapter One suggests, we never left our Source. We are really denying that we are still home, in the tree house, in heaven with God. This earthly reality is but a dream, and belief in **it** as Reality is denial.

Embracing our pain

How do we stop this denial? Most of us do not recognize that we have become addicted to pain. We hide from our pain which is how most addictions begin. We must stop this pattern. Only then can we feel, embrace, and surrender to our pain. (Please refer to the three-step process "Feeling our feelings" in the chapter Ten). By feeling and embracing our pain, we can stop covering it with some other substance or activity. We then are able to deal with the pain that is our underlying addiction.

Many compulsive overeaters say that they always feel "empty" inside (just another word for pain), and that they use food to fill their emptiness. Food doesn't work of course but they continue to eat because they believe that will fill their emptiness. We use many substances in the same way, attempting to fill a hole with alcohol, drugs, sex, and even shopping. The emptiness comes from our feeling of separation, however, and *no thing* will ever fill this hole.

Imagine that this addictive process is like a Boston Cream Pie. At the bottom of the pie we have a chocolate cookie crust, covered with cream and chocolate and all the other ingredients. You cannot see much of the cookie crust at the bottom, since it is buried beneath the other ingredients—all of the goo. All of these other ingredients are our layers of the addictions. It does not matter what you call these layers, because their only function is to cover pain. We eat, drink, purchase, gamble, and work, to cover the pain and fill the hole that we feel inside ourselves. We don't want to face this pain, but healing any addiction begins with admitting that we do feel and experience pain. We can heal our particular addiction or addictions once we acknowledge this. *We must do this before we can heal the addiction that we have to the separation from our Source.*

First we must determine our addictions. As I suggested above you may not have an obvious addiction to food, cigarettes, drugs, or shopping, or perhaps you may not be aware of having any addictions. My experience in counseling has shown me that most of us have compulsive-obsessive behavior patterns, however: worrying, obsessive house cleaning, concern for others, fear of what others think of us, a need for success, an obsessive need to be accepted and loved. One that came up recently in a session was an addiction to needing to be right all the time. This person was petrified of being wrong, no matter what the circumstance. She **had** to be right. As much as I don't like to admit it, I for one can relate to that particular trait. One of my favorite lines from *A Course in Miracles* is "Do you prefer that you be right or happy?"[3]

We must identify these mental, physical, and emotional patterns before we can feel at peace with ourselves. We then can work on healing and releasing them, and begin choosing new healthy patterns in their place.

12-Step Programs

12-Step meetings can be very beneficial in this initial stage of discovering and releasing our obsessive patterns. These meetings help us to identify our addictive patterns and support us in achieving a state of balance, which allows us to release and move beyond the addiction.

There are many such programs, and it should not be difficult to find one where you feel comfortable. When we uncover and acknowledge our specific addictions, we are no longer at their mercy. We can look at them instead with love and find balance within ourselves. As we release ourselves from the addiction, we begin working on self-love and self-esteem. We fill ourselves with our Higher Power, rather than a substance or an old behavior.

12-step programs are effective in part because they are spiritual programs, putting great emphasis on a Higher Power. They are not "religious" per se, since they do not suggest or determine what your Higher Power should be. You discover and determine that for yourself.

In my own experience, 12-step programs provide invaluable gifts. Here are a few:

1. They provide a safe and nurturing environment where I can admit to myself, my Higher Power, and others that I am powerless over my addiction. They provide a supportive place to come to terms with my denial.

2. They provide a safe place where I can share what is going on in my life without being judged.

3. Everyone in these meetings talks about the same patterns, and therefore there is very little judgment. I realized that I was not the only one with destructive behavior patterns, and this was very comforting.

4. Because there is very little judgment, we allow ourselves to experience grace. Grace in turn equals forgiveness. These meetings thus provide an opportunity to forgive others, and to feel forgiveness from others.

5. This increases one's self-esteem. This step is absolutely necessary, to discontinue destructive patterns. The meetings provide an opportunity for increased self-love and self-esteem.

6. I am not alone in my healing process. It takes great willingness and support to heal an addictive behavior. Since we are not separate from one another in Truth, healing in a group atmosphere is very powerful, and is easier than doing it alone.

(Note: I have recommended in the course of counseling to many people that they attend particular 12-step meetings. They often have identified their own specific addictions, but they resist going to even one meeting. If you resist attending a 12-step program, you could be denying your addiction, or denying that you need to act upon it. Resistance creates persistence; the degree to which one resists is related to the degree to which the person wants to maintain pain.)

For many, 12-step programs become a large part of their life. Many alcoholics credit Alcoholics Anonymous with saving their lives, and they continue to use the tools of the program and attend meetings throughout their lives. For many, the program also becomes their spiritual home and family, a source of friends and recreation.

Beyond labels

We next must move beyond the labels of our individual addictions. We need to move beyond *all* labels, because all labels separate. This is easy to see among religious groups: Fundamentalist Christians create separation from New Agers, who separate from Catholics, who feel separate from Muslims and so forth. Labels in themselves are actually not a problem; the problem arises when we identify the label with who we think we are. That belief separates us from one another. Remember, we name an addictive behavior so that we can release it. Addictive behavior blocks love's awareness. It thus becomes important to release our identification with the label **after** we heal from the destructive addictive behavior.

I forget the Truth when I confuse my addictive behavior with who I am. At the very core of our Beingness, we are love, joy, and peace. Our *behavior* is addictive, and that is what we claim when we say we "are alcoholic" or we "are addicts." I do not see that distinction made with many addicts, however. Instead, I often hear, "I am an addict or an alcoholic; that is what or who I am." **That** is denial. **That** is the label we must move beyond. Yes, I am powerless over alcohol; yes, I once practiced alcoholic behavior. But **I am** a whole, perfect, loving child of my Higher Power, God. We only treat ourselves as separate, different, and unique, when we identify our labels with who we are, rather than a particular behavior.

I once attended an open AA meeting that included a visitor who was a member of, Gamblers Anonymous.* He shared the extreme difficulty he had in healing his gambling addiction, and suggested that it was more difficult than healing an alcohol addiction. You can imagine what happened next. Some people at the meeting took up the gauntlet and started to explain why it was much harder to quit drinking than gambling. The meeting became very tense, which in my experience was unusual, and with an obvious commitment to separation. The self-defeating attitude that **my** addiction is more difficult to overcome than **yours**, simply creates an additional sense of separation. All addictions are difficult to break. If we treat one as more difficult to break than another, we are lying to ourselves and using the addiction label to "Identify" ourselves.

---

* "Open" AA meetings are open to any member of the public who wishes to attend. "Closed" AA meetings are open to those who meet *"[t]he only requirement for membership...a desire to stop drinking."* Alcoholics Anonymous, Tradition Three.

We all want to be "special." We all want to be unique and different. Out of low self-esteem, we try to be better than someone else, and therefore "special." One of the ways we can try to be "special" is to make our addiction special, which happens when we actively use an addictive substance. Most addicts have a special relationship with their drug of choice. Many consider the substance to be their best and sometimes only, friend. For many, the substance becomes their "higher power." We can make our addiction "special" even in recovery, by making it a more difficult addiction to overcome. This attitude supports the ego's purpose, which is to continue the separation—through a special relationship with the substance or addictive behavior in this case.

The danger in identifying yourself by a label

We have not moved beyond the addiction if we continue to use a label to separate even though we may not be practicing addictive behavior. We must graduate from the need for labels as a way to identify ourselves. This belief keeps us feeling separate from one another and our Higher Power. Remember, our beliefs determine our world as well as our self-image. Using a label does not support my remembering the truth of who I am. In recovery we must honor where we are right now and what we need right now, and we must take the necessary steps to support ourselves. We must look at the underlying beliefs that we have about ourselves and each other before we can experience freedom in our lives.

12-step programs are incredibly powerful and extremely beneficial. They help us to see our addictive behavior. They help us to look at the layers in the Boston Cream pie that cover the cookie crust—the underlying addiction of pain. I am *not* suggesting, therefore, that we pretend not to have addictive behavior. That is only another form of denial. Alcoholics and addicts must label themselves as such in the initial stages of recovery so that they can recognise their addictive bahavior and then release themselves from it. I *am* suggesting that we must move beyond identifying *ourselves* as the label.

We will change our conscious awareness about ourselves and each other when we recover from our individual addictions and love ourselves. This new awareness will change every area of our lives. What used to feel comfortable and good, won't any longer. It doesn't feel good to abuse ourselves when we love ourselves. It doesn't feel good to get fuzzy in the head from wine. It doesn't feel good to overeat. It just doesn't feel good, so we simply discontinue doing it.

In the same way, we will reach a point in our life where pain just doesn't make any sense, where we have had enough of it and we no longer choose to be addicted to it. This means that we feel less guilty. The more we love ourselves, the less punishment we feel we deserve, and the less pain we will inflict upon ourselves. Many of us are very close to that point now. More often we choose not having pain over having pain. We choose things that support living a pain- free life. This is a step by step process.

A conversation about addiction

(The following is transcript of a conversation between a client and myself):

Carol: I have a belief that nothing works for me. On every level and with all sorts of different things. The stuff I learn at church, at my 12-step meetings—I hear myself saying this stuff won't work for me. But then I don't work it.

Pamela: That is an excellent form of sabotage.

Carol: Yes, I thought it was pretty clever.

Pamela: If you have the affirmation that "Nothing works for me," that will absolutely manifest in your life. That also sounds like an easy affirmation to change.

Carol: Okay, but if it is something that is really deeply ingrained, does it take a lot of work to let it go? Or, can it be easy? Can I choose not to let this be my truth anymore?

P.: We are programmed by the belief system that says: "It is very simple but it isn't easy. "Why do we continue to believe that? Why can't we change our minds and believe that it is easy?

C.: I always thought this fed into my belief system about myself, that I wasn't worthy, so why should anything work for me?

P.: Yes, that is a perfect form of sabotage. Okay, so why don't you ask now, to feel worthy. Give yourself permission to feel worthy.

C.: But, if I let go of that one, then I can't be addicted to pain— so I have been looking at that lately, at how I really am addicted to pain, and how I choose to be in painful situations.

P.: One of the things that I have found interesting in my process about releasing pain is that in my 12-step programs, I would do a 4th and a 5th step. (*"Step 4: Made a searching and fearless moral inventory of ourselves. Step 5: Admitted to God, to ourselves and to another human being the exact nature of our wrongs."*) But, then I would never do a 6th and a 7th step. (*"Step 6: Were entirely ready to have God remove all these defects of character. Step 7: Humbly asked Him to remove our shortcomings."*) I never did the 6th and 7th because I wasn't entirely ready to be released from the pain. It is really important to ask your Higher Power for this help. The human part of you has a major investment in keeping you stuck in your destructive behavior patterns, because if you do not stay stuck in them you are going to leave your human (sinful) self behind.

C.: So the fear I feel about the change, comes from my human part, and it knows that it works for me, and that I am fearful about changing.

P.: Yes. Your human mind knows how good you are at sabotaging yourself in your progress which is why we choose the same dysfunctional behavior patterns over and over again. They work, and we have become very good at our dysfunctional patterns. It has become a fail-safe for the ego. Why try to figure out a new pattern when we already have one that works—at least in the ego's mind.

C.: But ultimately God is going to help me out here?

P.: Yes, that's right. What you have to remember is that you are an extension of God and you must open yourself to allowing God's assistance to be available to you.

C.: When I think about God, I still see God as outside of myself. I'm working on that: feeling God within me.

P.: I understand. Let's remember that is the bottom line addiction: to feel separate from God and pretend that we are indeed separate from God. So you can approach addiction in a number of different ways depending upon what works for you and what you resist least. For me, working on the obvious addictions that I had, to substances, to relationships, to work, was a lot easier than working on the addiction of feeling separate from God, because I could stop the substance abuse, stop acting out in a relationship addiction and find balance in my work. But finding that state of balance only came through loving myself, and working the 12 steps and getting a higher sense of self esteem. And this is why the 12-

step programs are absolutely invaluable in helping us work through our addictions. 12-step programs give us grace and self-esteem as well as helping us move through the addictions that we know we have.

These two gifts, grace and self-esteem are absolutely vital in the recovery process. Without the gift of grace, which the 12-step program helps you become aware of, and without self-esteem, how could you remember that God is inside of you? The lack of self-esteem encourages you to push God even further away. Why would God want to have anything to do with me because I am so lowly? This is why it is easier for many people to work on the addictions that they know they already have, before addressing the underlying addiction to the separation.

Exercises

1. Look at your life and your behavior patterns. Identify where you may be denying a possible addiction.

2. If you are currently aware of your addictions, do not punish yourself for your addictive tendencies. We all have them—it is part of the human condition.

3. If you are aware of your addictions and are not currently in a support group, try one! Go at least six times, and try different groups. Give the process a chance.

4. If you have been active in a 12-step program for at least five years, look carefully at your beliefs about the program. Look at how you identify yourself. Do you identify yourself with the label for your addiction, or do you understand that it is the behavior you are identifying?

5. Identify yourself only as a reflection of your Higher Power. Name and Claim the Truth about Yourself!

14

The world is a safe place— It's All an Ego System

" What's the meaning of a flower? There's a Zen story about a sermon of the Buddha in which he simply lifted a flower. There was only one man who gave him a sign with his eyes that he understood what was said. Now, the Buddha himself is called "the one thus come." There's no meaning. What's the meaning of the universe? What's the meaning of a flea? It's just there. That's it. And your own meaning is that you're there. We're so engaged in doing things to achieve purposes of outer value that we forget that the inner value, the rapture that is associated with being alive, is what it's all about."[1]

—Joseph Campbell

A few years ago as I was planning a trip to Ohio to give the talk "Forgiveness, a Key to Abundance," I got sick. I had strep throat and a viral infection culminating in total laryngitis. Obviously I could not work, and I was forced to cancel the talk and a playshop.

Canceling this engagement allowed me the opportunity to **forgive myself** for being sick and canceling the engagement. But, you may ask, why should anyone feel guilty for getting sick? Let's get to that a little later.

During this time of illness I had the most incredible realization. One morning I got up feeling a bit better. I had been sick about a week and was taking penicillin. My body reacts strongly to drugs. In fact, the body tries to reject and eliminate the drug, causing even more stress on the body, which is already trying to heal itself. So I felt quite a bit better until I took the penicillin, and then I felt really tired again. Before I went back to bed though, I finally understood something that I hadn't before. I am sure you can relate to knowing something intellectually for quite some time before finally **getting it**. You **know** it. Well, this morning, **I got it** about illness. I finally understood that illness is meaningless.

I realize that this is going to fly in the face of metaphysical and psychological teachings. But we often teach one thing and practice another. In this case, we teach that everything is part of God, the creative force of love. We also teach that the world is inherently neutral: there is no good, there is no bad, there is *only* the meaning that *we* give to things. Let that sink in a little, because this can be a really huge change in perception. All our life, we have been taught that everything has meaning, and we have been taught to seek out that meaning.

The world is a neutral place

Looking at the world as a neutral place is like looking at a blank wall and understanding the wall encompasses all the meaning that there is in the world. There is nothing else. I did not like this when I first heard it. I got very depressed. I asked, "What do you mean, there is no meaning in the world? There has to be meaning. There has to be something that means something! Doesn't there?" I didn't want to believe this concept, and I let go of the idea. With that I also let go of studying *A Course in Miracles* which says that the world as we perceive it is meaningless:

"I am upset because I see a meaningless world."

" The importance of this idea lies in the fact that it contains a correction for a major perceptual distortion. You think that what upsets you is a frightening world, or a sad world, or a violent world, or an insane world. All these attributes are given it by you. The world is meaningless in itself."[2]

A couple of years later I picked up the book again. I came to this section, and again I became depressed over the fact that the world is meaningless. But *A Course in Miracles* says that if we *only* see the world as meaningless, we will indeed become depressed: *"A meaningless world engenders fear."*[3] It also states that *"**God** did not create a meaningless world."*[4] The world we currently perceive is not the world that God created. We only see our perception of that world, and provide all of its meaning. For that reason, we must be careful in choosing that meaning. In hindsight, I felt exactly what the *Course* predicted. I was upset because I saw a meaningless world.

The morning, that I took the penicilin, I understood this concept in a different way. I felt elated: "Hooray, the world is meaningless, that is so wonderful, because that means I am totally free, and so are you, to give every event that ever happens to you the meaning that you want to give it. It gives you total freedom in the world. You no longer need to be a victim or at the mercy of anything, including illness."

We used to ask "What did I do wrong?" when we became ill. "I'm guilty; I did something wrong, and I have to pay for my sins." "God is punishing me." (I'm really glad that I don't believe that one any longer!) Those who have studied metaphysics look at the subject of illness in yet another way: "What does this mean?" I have a sore throat. Well, what does that mean? I hurt my knees. Well, what do knees mean in the metaphysical context? There are books out there that tell you organ for organ, bone for bone, muscle for muscle, illness for illness what it all means in the metaphysical system.

That's okay, if you want to play this game. But it is all a game, an ego game. I have known this for a long time, but the other morning I **got** it at another level. "So I got sick… So what?" I could make up all sorts of reasons why. Maybe I didn't want to go to Ohio. Maybe this, maybe that.

Egyptians believed that you were "possessed" by a demonic spirit when you became ill, and they would bring a priest to expel the spirit. They believed that you wouldn't recover unless this spirit was expelled. We have come a long way since then. Metaphysics appears to offer a more reasonable belief system, focusing on how I created this reality and what lessons I am trying to learn. But the metaphysical system is still an ego system, because blaming ourselves for creating an illness, or using illness to teach ourselves lessons, is just another way to avoid remembering the truth about who and what we really are.

I believe that our guilt causes our illnesses. Illness becomes another way to punish ourselves. The metaphysical system for explaining our various illnesses is just another ego system. Analysis is one of the ego's favorite pastimes, and analyzing the reasons for our illness perpetuates the game and makes it seem very real, especially since we identify so heavily with our body.

Every system is an ego system

Every system out there is an ego system: Catholicism, democracy, communism, *A Course in Miracles*, Science of the Mind, Unity, Baptist, Presbyterian, Unitarian, Fundamentalism—all of them are ego systems. None is more or less correct than another. They are all aspects of the game of life; you can choose to play any of them. One could also say that they are all variations on a ride in the amusement park.

I don't know if any of you were ever "seekers of truth." I remember when I used to seek truth. I would go to different workshops, each time thinking that the workshop would provide the truth. I was going to learn the final, ultimate truth and then, I would be illuminated. I finally realized, though, that every workshop is another ego system. I am not implying that these tools are not helpful; they are. If we understand that each one is based on the ego, however, we can appreciate the gifts that each provides and stop judging one as better than another.

Frankly, I don't know how to live in this world without interacting with ego systems, unless I live in a cave. A friend recently shared a cartoon with me. It had two pictures, one of a guru sitting in his cave with the caption "OM," and one of a cow with the caption "Moo." What is the difference whether we OM or we Moo? Probably none. The point is we can really get into trouble when we take the ego systems seriously.

Understanding that the world is inherently meaningless means that we are free to give it whatever meaning we want. We do this through joining together in the thoughts about the world that we hold in common.

We can choose to see the world as a safe place, blessed, harmonious, beautiful and health-filled. If we give it that meaning, that is what it will become. We have concentrated on world peace, and in many areas of the world that is happening. When we focus our attention on what we want, that is the meaning that we will give to the planet.

My being sick allowed me to examine the meaning that I usually give to illness. This time I decided not to give it any meaning. Maybe I won't be sick anymore, maybe I will, but **not** empowering the illness with meaning gives me the freedom *not* to feel guilty.

The law of the ego: Seek but do not find

Analysis is a by-product of the search for hidden meanings, and analysis is the ego's game. *A Course in Miracles* points out that one of the favorite laws of the ego says *"Seek but do not find?"*[5] This shows us the insanity of ego systems. We can see this law in action in many areas of our life, such as romantic love. How many of you are seeking but not finding relationships? Or you have found a relationship, but are not quite sure that this is really **the** one, playing it safe and keeping your options open? We always find *something* wrong with whatever we choose. This is part of seeking but not finding. When we let go of analysis and allow our lives to flow, wonderful gifts will come to us without our seeking them out.

I encourage you to look at the meaning that you give to everything in your life. Discover where you give meanings that keep you from experiencing your good. Find out what belief systems you hold that do not support you, and change them. You control your life because it is a blank screen. You decide the movie that you want to play on your blank screen. You are the producer, the director and the star. Further, since everyone is your mirror, you play all the roles in your movie, and at the same time you are the viewer. You play the hero or heroine and the role of the villain. I know a lot of us don't like being the villain. We want to play the "good guy," but I guarantee you that there is someone in this world for whom you are the villain.

We create our own reality, as we discussed in Chapter Five. We create our reality by giving meaning to the world. The world simply reflects the beliefs we hold about it, and that is how we will experience it. We have chosen to perceive this world as a dark and dangerous place since our initial choice in the tree house. This is a very important concept to understand. We create our own realities. We create and recreate our world every moment of every day, with every thought that we think. And when we finally choose to see the world as safe, beautiful, peace-filled, and abundant, that is how it will be for us. That puts us in a pretty powerful position. We either join together in thoughts based on fear about the world, which will create for us a fear-filled world, or we join in seeing a world of beauty and peace, based in love. This will allow us to see the Truth, the meaning that the Creator gave to the world.

In other words, you will see and experience a safe, happy, joyous, healthy playground in this world, if you align with Truth. Believe the world to be safe, and it will be; believe the world to be unsafe, and it will be. You are in charge.

My husband had a great experience that illustrates that he is the producer/director of his world. He was vacationing for a month in Seville, Spain in a house in the middle of the city. While there, he read *Illusions* [6] by Richard Bach. In the story a vampire-type character suddenly appears in the field where Richard Bach and Donald Shimoda are spending the night with their biplanes. This was a scary experience for Richard, and Donald explains that we attract all events in our lives. All experiences hold gifts within them, and we seek out challenging experiences for those gifts. Donald later takes Richard to see the movie *Butch Cassidy and the Sundance Kid*. The purpose of taking him to the movie and attracting the vampire was to explain that our lives are in fact like a movie, and that we are the producer/director.

Patrick decided to go out for a walk after reading this section of the book. A man dressed in black came up to him with a knife and attempted to rob him. Patrick yelled at the top of his lungs and ran from the attacker. This experience had a very profound impact on him, happening as it did just after reading that particular section in the book. It was as if his Higher Power was proving this concept by giving him an experience very much like the one in the book.

Equally important to understand is that you are continually recreating your image of yourself while you recreate your world. Your beliefs about yourself determine who you are and which roles that you decide to play. If you believe yourself to be a "good" person, that is most likely how you will be perceived. If you believe less-than-loving thoughts about yourself, that is how you will be perceived by yourself and others, so that you can recognize and release these unloving beliefs about yourself.

Most of us believe that we are a combination of good and bad. Carl Jung describes the bad as our "shadow self;" we also could call this side of ourselves the "villain" or the "ego." The ego is that part of ourselves that believes that we are separate from God, that we are less than loving, that we are sinful or bad.

I once had a very vivid dream that explained my relationship with my ego or villain self.

The Ego and I: a dream

One night I dreamed that I had a daughter. She appeared to be in her twenties, and was quite tall, strong, and rather beautiful. I remember thinking that I was truly surprised to have a daughter who looked so beautiful. She accompanied me much of the time and we took long walks together. She began to interact with people in a violent manner, sometimes doing incredibly horrific things. One time, for example, we were walking down a street talking, and she walked up to a person and ate off his face. Another time she put her hands on the top of a person's head and tore him in half. It was unbelievable to me, but she did this with great ease and little regret.

I didn't know what to do. Here was my child, to whom I had given life, committing outrageous acts of violence. I felt the need to protect her and destroy her simultaneously. I thought: "How do I destroy my own child?"

One day, feeling that I could no longer allow her to continue her destructive behavior, I decided to trick her. I saw a policeman and tried to figure out a way to have her arrested. Again, though, I had mixed feelings. She was my child; how could I be responsible for destroying her, even though I knew how destructive and unloving she appeared? I was ready to protect her by keeping her safely hidden, when she attacked the policeman. Suddenly I found myself with his gun in my hand; it was large and heavy. I aimed at her, but I could not pull the trigger. I tried again, but it wouldn't budge. I didn't feel strong enough. My finger just could not pull the trigger.

The policeman however, somehow stopped my daughter's attack without using physical force. She looked at me with confusion in her eyes as she surrendered to the policeman; it seemed as though she melted and became fluid.

Interpretation

This dream definitely symbolized my relationship with my ego. In this dream, my daughter represented my ego (or villain self).

She often accompanied me, attacking others viciously with little regret. Even so, I clearly remember wanting to protect and defend her. The fact that my ego appeared in this dream as my daughter is extremely revealing. It explains our deep allegiance to our ego. At a very deep level, we know that we gave life to it. (Actually, to the belief in it, because in the truest sense of reality, the ego is not real). We feel as though it is our child—an extension of us—to be protected at all costs. We defend it no matter its actions, including its outrageous destruction of others.

The feelings in this dream were very strong: protect or kill her; confusion; run away with and hide the ego. My dilemma is whether I should destroy, hide, or imprison a part of myself. I have often read about the need to kill the ego, which is ludicrous. How do you kill something that is not real? However, I protect and defend my ego beliefs every day. I try to hide from it, or hide it from others. Part of my reluctance in writing this book is due in part to my not wanting you to see the ego games that I play. Part of me wants you to believe that I as a minister and teacher have it all together, all the time. I wish!

Pretending that my daughter is my ego separates the ego from me. (This is the same as believing that we are separate from our Higher Power.) I did not see myself viciously attacking another; I saw my daughter committing the acts of violence. I remember when my younger brother would say "The devil made me do it" when he got in trouble. We cannot be blamed for our ego's behavior if it is something outside of ourselves. We pass the buck to the ego. We blame our behavior on anyone besides ourselves, even if this "anyone" isn't real.

As I continue to ponder the dream's symbolism, I see the policeman as a Higher Power, an authority figure, perhaps that part of myself that does know the truth. It is interesting that his gun would not fire, so that I could not kill my daughter. She (and I) ultimately surrendered to this figure, and she melted. Melting equals liquefying, losing the ability to attack, becoming fluid, losing structure, loosing form.

As I surrender to my Higher Power, to the God within me, I surrender my belief in an ego, and it loses its power. It loses its hold over me. As we surrender, we lose our belief that the villains in the world are somehow separate from us. As we embrace the ego or the villain in each of us, eventually we see it as the game it is. Jung suggested that we face our shadow self, since hiding from it only increases its imaginary hold upon us. The villain is simply playing a role. At the end of my dream there was no struggle and no physical force, just some confusion and then melting. I believe that it is that simple. All I need do is to be willing to surrender to God, my Higher Power. I don't need to know how; my Higher Power knows, and it will do all that needs to be done. I need only be willing. Acceptance of the ego is part of the process of the surrender.

Many play the role of villain: Hitler, Judas, Saddam Hussein, as well as common thieves, car hijackers, and child molesters. We tend to separate ourselves from these characters. We judge them and hold ourselves superior to them. But, my dream tells me that I am not separate from them; we are one. In their own way they are heroes too, for they bring us many opportunities (gifts) to see the beliefs we hold that no longer support us.

With this freeing concept, I concluded that from now on I will give only supportive meaning to situations, others, and myself. Why give any other meaning? Why **make** yourself feel guilty? Guilt is part of the "seek and do not find" game. Remember, the only two methods of relating with one another on this planet are: 1. We demonstrate love; 2. We ask for it. And remember, it is **all a game.** The first book I read when I studied metaphysics was *The Game of Life and How to Play it* by Florence Shovel Shinn. This wonderful book emphasizes that we really are participants in a game that we call life. This is your life—how do you want to play it? What are the meanings that you give this game? "Life is hard and then you die?" "It takes HARD work to get ahead?" (Ahead where? And for what?) "He who has the most toys when he dies wins?" (What does he win? Does he take his toys with him?)

How do we live in a safe world?

How do we live in a safe world? How do we create that reality? The solution is to choose for love, to choose to make decisions with God, to choose to be happy. These choices assist us in seeing the Truth behind the illusion of the unsafe world, the Truth behind the illusion of fear, hatred, poverty, and war. When we choose from a place of fear or limitation, when we think the world is real and fixed, we become locked within the illusion. We think we are its victims. We forget that it is a game, and that as its creators and players we can change the game at any time.

The only change we need to make is at the level of thought

A remarkable new theory of reality holds that the universe is a giant hologram, containing matter and consciousness. David Bohm (a protégé of Einstein) and neurophysiologist Karl Pribram of Stanford University, two of the world's most eminent scientists, believe that the universe itself may be an image or construct created, at least in part, by the human mind.

> *" Our brains mathematically construct objective reality by interpreting frequencies that are ultimately projections from another dimension, a deeper order of existence that is beyond both space and time: The brain is a hologram enfolded in a holographic universe."*[7]

This new way of looking at the universe explains many mysterious phenomena such as telepathy, near-death experiences, mystical experiences—many of the concepts that we have been discussing throughout this book. This concept supports that what we think creates our reality, and creates it at a very fundamental and specific level.

We must become responsible for our thoughts. To create a safe world we need to see the world through loving eyes, rather than judging eyes. Our world will then transform in the twinkling of an eye. When we look to the world for our safety, we are looking in the wrong place. Our safety comes instead from the understanding that the world is inside of us, not outside, and from remembering the truth of who we are—the perfect, indestructible extensions of Love.

Earth Changes

I should mention the topic of "natural disasters" here. As we approach the millennia, several books and TV programs dedicated to prophecies by such notables as Nostradamus have appeared. Psychics and various newsletters predict upcoming catastrophic events. These predictions arise from the perception of the world as an unsafe place. They come from choosing to see the world through the eyes of fear.

I received the following guidance in 1993:

"Be not afraid of earth changes, for indeed there is nothing to fear outside of you, as there is "nothing" outside of you. Many have decided to increase the velocity of the roller coaster syndrome. They desire larger and scarier roller coaster rides—thus they will make them for themselves. Each person lives in his/her own holographic universe. No two are exactly alike. So each determines his/her own reality through individual choices, i.e., belief systems. One can change belief systems any time, and move in and out of and around one another's realities."

It is always your choice

It is up to you whether or not you choose to ride on roller coasters. It is up to you whether you view the roller coaster ride as fearful or as an exciting experience to be savored. Every experience you have is yours to perceive, either from a place of fear or an understanding that all is in Perfect Order. You determine what is happening to you by the beliefs you hold and the judgments you make.

I recently saw a client who felt very victimized by the world, in particular her job. She had attempted to sue her boss for sexual harassment. She hired a lawyer who obtained many depositions from fellow employees (who were later fired). The lawyer then improperly filed the suit, handling it so poorly that there appeared to be no hope to get a "fair" trial. She now felt victimized by her employer, the lawyer, and the court system. She wrote a letter to her boss stating her feelings, was writing to her attorney protesting her treatment, and wanted to write to President Clinton to inform him of the harassment problems at this company. She said: "We have laws in this country that are supposed to work. I want the system to work!" She was looking to the world for her safety. I can understand her desire for fairness, and her expectation that our laws should work. But, laws were created as defense mechanisms that upheld the way certain people wanted things to be. Laws were made to protect the interests of specific individuals.

There would never be a need for laws if we always came from a space of love. Our system is based on chaos, because it is based upon a need to defend. A defense is the same as an attack, and thus our systems of law and order are designed to keep us attacking one another, to keep us separate, to keep us in fear. Why would we need laws, unless we believed something "bad" could happen? Our entire system is based on fear. Ask yourself: how could a system based on fear work? We can't expect our legal system to work when it is based entirely on blame. Our governments can't run efficiently when they were created to rule, dominate, and defend. A system rooted in fear is also rooted in insanity, and the system will operate insanely. It has to—what is born of chaos will be chaos.

My client is well meaning, but her desire for the laws to work is impossible. She wants laws to protect her, but protect her from what? From the dangerous men in her work place? When we choose to see danger, it will be there. When we choose to need protection, we will see something against which we need protect. Whatever we choose to perceive will appear for us. Our world is a giant hologram. It is an extension of our mind, our thoughts made into lifelike, life-size images that interact with one another. The only way to change the world is to change our minds. We are mistaken in believing that our laws will protect us, that we need laws at all. It comes back to this: choose from a place of fear and you will have to choose again. Choose from love and your world will bloom into the garden of Eden: safe, beautiful, abundant, and serene. It takes practice, but it's worth it.

Our initial choice to stay in the tree house is the only choice we need to change. Our choice from the perspective of the child in the tree house will always be made from fear. Although our manmade rules don't work and never will, we are never in any danger. We are simply choosing to stay in the tree house. Remember the idea of the amusement park ride? My client was riding a roller coaster that is only as scary as she believes it to be. Nothing here can really hurt us, because nothing here is truly real. We are here for a brief time, like a day in Disney World. It seems longer, and it seems scary and real, but that is part of the ride.

In truth, we are always safe. We can live in harmony, joy and bliss when we stop taking this place, our lives, our work, our rules here so seriously. We can play in this amusement park with the entire cast and crew until, weary at the end of the day, we recognize that it is time to go home. We leave the rides behind, we make a choice to end the game, we climb down from the tree house, walk across the patio, and remember the truth of our Beingness: Love.

The answer for this client is to practice forgiveness, for it is through forgiveness that she will understand that she is safe, and that she has nothing to fear from her boss, her attorney, or anyone else. When she forgives, she will recognize her choice to be on this particular ride, and she will choose to step off. Eventually she will understand that she was in truth never in danger, and never harmed, only playing a part in her drama of the moment.

Lesson #22 in the workbook of *A Course in Miracles* states this point clearly:

"What I see is a form of vengeance."

     " The world I see is hardly the
     representation of loving thoughts.
     It is a picture of attack on
     everything by everything. It is
     anything but a reflection of the

Love of God and the love of His
Son. It is my own attack thoughts
that give rise to this picture. My
loving thoughts will save me from
this perception of the world, and
give me the peace God intended me
to have." [8]

When we understand that the universe is totally neutral, with only the meaning that we give it, it becomes much easier to respond to the various challenges we choose to experience.

The programming out there rules our life. Start a journal. Each night for ten to fifteen minutes write about what you did during the day, and look at the belief systems you have that keep you stuck. Look to where your life is not flowing, and examine the belief system you have about that. Sometimes, after working hard to let go of a particular way of thinking or an old habit, we believe that we are free of the old pattern, only then to find that we still have it.

Soon after canceling my trip to Ohio, I was talking with a friend and what came out of my mouth was "You know, it is hard to get bookings." I heard that and said "OOPS, what just came out of my mouth?" When I initially started to tour, it seemed to be difficult to get bookings, because no one knew who I was. Now it is easy, because I have a large resume and an excellent reputation. Still, in my mind I believed that it is hard to get bookings. When I heard it come out of my mouth, I realized that I still believed that, and that this belief still affected my career. I was still living in the past rather than the present when I picked up the phone to get a booking. This illustrates that you can have contradicting belief systems at the same time. You move into a new belief that supports you while still holding a conflicting belief that is your saboteur. The saboteur could be the more powerful of the two beliefs, if you are not careful.

A man was raised in a very strict religion that forbade many simple things, such as dancing. As the man grew up, so the story goes, he let go of his old religious beliefs and adopted a much more gentle perception of God. He got married, and he and his wife loved to go dancing. Every time he went dancing, however, there would be some repercussion. He would get sick afterward; he would trip and fall leaving the dance; and other similar annoying consequences. One day he looked at why these things were happening, and remembered that dancing was considered a sin in his religion. He still held this belief at a deep subconscious level; instead of God punishing him, he was punishing himself. He let go of the old belief once he understood this and began enjoying his weekly dancing without any side effects.

It is very important to discover where you still hold old beliefs that don't support you. Different beliefs about something will cancel each other out, leaving the deepest and oldest belief. You can easily change sabotaging thoughts, because you created them in the first place, or perhaps bought them from someone else. I also find it helpful to look at the things we do with a sense of humor. If we didn't laugh at ourselves, we might really believe that we were in trouble.

I find it equally helpful to remember that everything in our lives is there for a purpose. Just because events do not have inherent meaning does not mean that each does not support us. Each event regardless of its meaning helps us to remember the truth about ourselves.

Exercise

Start a daily journal. Every night write for ten to fifteen minutes about your day. Record not only the events but also the feelings you had. Look for the patterns that run your life. What meaning did you give to events or people? Do you like that meaning, or do you wish to change it? What roles did you play during the day? Were you the hero or heroine, a bit player, or perhaps the villain? Look at this with amusement.

15

Everyone is My Savior

Did you know that everyone is your Savior? Did you
know that you are the Savior of the world? Did you
know that you can decide when we (all of us)
change our minds about who and what we really are? I have
talked and written a lot about the end of separation, and I
take this quite literally. Soon we will move into a state of
conscious awareness when we remember that we are One,
not separate individuals. You and I are the "I AM." We are
the Christ consciousness. We "see," "feel," "hear," and
"know" (understand) our oneness in this new state of consciousness. This won't just be a thought—it will be very real.

Most of us hold two very different and conflicting ideas
about ourselves: we are the divine children of God as well as
"human beings." Being "human" usually means being fal-
lible, weak, capable of mistakes, and even sinful. I remember my dad's excuse when he would go out on a binge: "I'm
only human." How can we be both of those things, a perfect
divine child of God and a sinful human being? This idea
causes confusion, as it should.

So which are we? Can we be both? If holding both ideas
causes conflict, giving up one might be a great idea. Which
do you keep? I believe that we are the perfect infinite children of God, that you and I are the "I AM," that we can remember this for ourselves and for everyone else.

Jesus did this. That is how he healed: he saw the perfection
in each of us so strongly that people were instantaneously

healed and even raised from the dead. A woman in our Wednesday night class stated: "If I believe that someone's pain is real, I'm allowing them to remain in their pain. But if I see their pain as illusion, I'm giving them permission to release the pain and their belief in it." When we acknowledge each other as human we maintain our belief in our frailty, confusion, and in sinfulness. When we acknowledge one another as each other's "Savior," on the other hand we see with our "real" eyes, those that Jesus and other great master teachers used.

Am I suggesting the denial of our humanness? Yes I am. Many of us have denied our humanness by attempting to be Super-human. Others have denied themselves through co-dependency and addictions. But this is simply the replacement of one egoic belief system for another. I am not suggesting that you deny that you *have* a body—that is simply another kind of aesthetic denial. What I am suggesting is that *you are not the body.* You are something far greater than you see yourself now. You are perfect and whole. *And it is within your power* to "save" the world from its erroneous beliefs about itself.

Imagine a world where each of us saw one another as our savior? Wow! It would be a different world. How do we do this on a daily basis?

Decide that everyone is your Savior

It does not matter if you believe this, or even understand it. Consciously allow this truth to be revealed to you. In 12-step programs we say: "Act as if." When we act as if something is true, we see it working in our lives. Opportunities present themselves for us to see the principle in action. People will treat us differently. Remember, what we focus on expands. When we see others as our savior, we empower them to be so. In effect, we give them permission. When we choose to recognize limitations, however, that is what we will see. As the saying goes, "Argue for your limitations and they are yours." Look at it another way: argue for another's limitations and they will be real in your eyes.

We will see the best in everyone when we make a conscious choice to understand that everyone is the savior of the world. We see them beyond the label "human." We give the gift of freedom, and we permit others (and therefore ourselves) to rise above our limiting beliefs.

In a classroom experiment teachers were given information concerning specific pupils in their classes. In some instances the teacher was told that particular children were extremely gifted, although these children had actually tested average for their age. The teachers perceived and treated the children as if they were extremely gifted, and the children responded as if they were. Their performance met their teachers' expectations. The children became what they were perceived to be. In another part of this experiment, children who had tested as exceptional were labeled as average or below average. Guess what their performance was? They were perceived by the teachers as not capable of doing the work, and that is how they responded.

This is a remarkable study. It shows us how our perception works. I am the one who needs to change **my** mind about who you are and your impact on my life. The choice to see, feel, and know that you are my savior is a powerful one.

People with whom I share this idea love it and want to see everyone as their savior. At the same time, they also argue for their limitations. I hear, "Okay, it is a great principle, but this person in my life has always acted this way. Let's face it, some people are just not reliable. Some people cannot be trusted. We just don't see eye to eye. How do I begin?"

Look for a common denominator between you and your "Savior."

What do you have in common? We often focus on how we are different from others, especially those with whom we feel conflict. We focus on what separates us, rather than what joins us. Looking for the common denominator means finding something we already agree upon: an idea, a concept, a belief. Sometimes this is easy; we feel very comfortable with those with whom we have a lot in common. Have you ever just met someone and felt as though you have known that person forever? Often this is because you have a lot in common with that person. At other times, though, we don't have this instant recognition. We then need to listen carefully and identify what we do have in common. How do I find that common denominator?

Listen

Listening is not a skill that many of us were taught, and as children, we rarely felt listened to. We must be willing to put aside our own ideas for the moment and devote all of our attention to the other person. This takes practice. It means that all we think about is what the other person is saying. We empty ourselves of ourselves, and *be there* for that person.

For many of us this is a magnificent step. We are giving a great gift to the person speaking, and to ourselves as well. This creates a very safe space for the person talking, and allows us to hear what is really being said. In the past, I thought of what I was going to say next, or how I disagreed, or how I was going to prove that I was right. In looking for the common denominator, we must be willing to stop needing to be right all the time. For some of us, needing to be right has become a major compulsion, and it will take some time to release it. Being aware that needing to be right can be a compulsion is a major step in letting go of the need to stay separate.

I once vacationed in Lake Tahoe with my mother. While there, my mom and I went to an arts and crafts fair. One of the booths had beautiful hand-painted shirts; since it was the closing afternoon, the artist was discounting all of her merchandise. My mom always loves a bargain, and the artist was a very convincing salesperson. She had one striking sweatshirt with gold, mauve, gray-blues, golden wings, a cross, and the word "Jesus" painted on it. My mom said "Oh, I must buy this for my daughter. She is a minister." Well, the woman immediately asked what denomination, which church, all the questions about the labels that determine how we are alike or how we are separate. I answered by saying that the focus of my ministry is to move beyond guilt and fear. Her reaction was "I think guilt is a very good thing." Clearly this woman and I had some basic differences in our belief systems, so I chose to leave it at that. I loved her shirts, including the Jesus sweatshirt, and I decided to stay with what we had in common.

Her husband overheard the conversation, however, and asked me to indulge him in a debate. I responded that I do not debate spiritual beliefs. He ignored that and suggested that guilt was a good thing. He likened it to a child touching a hot burner on a stove: guilt teaches us what is right and what is wrong. I smiled and listened; I knew that if I suggested that there was no "wrong" in the world, we would definitely find ourselves in opposing camps. I looked for what we had in common. I truly listened to this man. I acknowledged him, and let him know that he was truly being heard. At the same time, I consciously chose to recognize this man as my savior, and I patiently waited for what else he had to say.

His next sentence was: "I believe that everyone feels guilt; every person on the planet feels guilty." There it was: absolute agreement, a common denominator. I said, "I agree with you completely; everyone in the world feels guilty. But no one really wants to feel guilty, do you think?" He agreed. I continued: "So we try to give our guilt away. I don't want to feel guilty, so I try to give my guilt away to you. The way I try to do this is by trying to make you feel guilty. I try to unload it onto you. This may feel like it works for a brief time, but sooner or later I feel my guilt again and look for someone else to give it to. It becomes a never-ending process, and we are all left with our guilt." He looked at me and I could see the wheels in his head turning. He nodded saying, "Okay, I follow your line of thinking, keep going."

I asked for agreement in each of the next statements, so that if he disagreed, we could find some common ground again. "We are all the children of God, right?" "*Yes.*" "All of us, every person on the earth, right?" "*Yes.*" "No matter what we've done, from Hitler and Saddam Hussein to Mother Theresa, we are **all** children of God—**no one** excluded, right?" "*Right.*" "So we stop trying to give the guilt away by treating each other as the perfect children of God."

This brought me back to the initial step, one I need to take over and over again:

I consciously choose again to see this person as my savior

I looked into his eyes very purposefully and said: "You are the perfect child of God, and I need to treat you as such. It is by treating you as such that I remember the truth about you, which allows me to remember this about everyone else, including myself. That's all we need to do, love one another and remember the truth." He looked at me and said "I agree with everything you say. I can't find anything to disagree with."

This conversation was a tremendous gift, for it brought us into alignment with one another. We chose to see each other in our similarities. I was not there trying to teach, prove a point, or be right. I never for a moment felt as though I needed to defend anything. I was not trying to protect myself or my belief system. I was telling my truth, and I wanted to see this man as my savior, focusing on how we are the same, not separate. And it happened! No buttons were pushed; we held each other in high regard, and for that period of time we acknowledged our oneness as children of God.

It's okay to have different beliefs

I believe we can permit each other to have different beliefs without making each other wrong. We can understand that it is perfectly fine to disagree and to hold our own understandings. But we must remember that these beliefs are only perceptions that we hold or defend. Perceptions are always individual. In looking for the common denominators, we are asking to join, rather than stay separate.

At times we may think that the common denominator is hiding from us. This is the time to look at the next step.

I let go of the need to be right

Have you ever needed to be right? We all have at some time or another; some of us, myself included, *really* like being right. In fact the need to be right seems necessary for self-preservation, and we find it difficult to extricate ourselves from our position. We have been taught certain "Christian ethics" in our society, which are often seen as right and wrong. When we have a pair of opposites such as right and wrong, though, we tend to polarize ourselves. Most of us naturally want to be on the side of "right," because who wants to be "wrong?"

If I believe I am right and you disagree that makes you wrong. You probably don't want to be wrong, especially since "wrong" is associated with "bad" or "mistaken" or even "sinful." Both parties therefore will defend their positions because they want to be right rather than wrong. An example where we can easily see this behavior today is the issue of abortion. We have two diametrically opposed camps: the "right to life" people defending the rights of the newly conceived baby, and the "pro-choice" people who believe that it is the right of the woman to decide what is best for her own emotional and physical well-being. Each camp states that they are right and the other is wrong. Both camps use God to defend their side. We have seen the extent to which one will defend his/her position with violence and in several instances, murder.

Fear as the common denominator

How do we find a common denominator in this situation? We might discover that the only common denominator is **fear**. The right-to-life individuals fear for the lives and souls of the unborn children. The pro-choice people fear the loss of what they can or cannot do with their own bodies. Both sides fear the loss of something that they hold very dear. A solution may seem distant, but actually the important step is to identify the common denominator, in this case fear. Once we do that, we can understand that we are both on the same side, just with different views.

There is something we can physically do to assist in this process. Stand or sit side-by-side with someone while discussing an issue instead of sitting opposite one another. Imagine this: you would already be on the same side, looking at the issue from the same perspective, rather than sitting in a opposing posture. You are both facing the same direction. It may sound silly, but it really works and is a very powerful tool.

Imagine two people holding radically different opinions but willing to discuss their beliefs without defending their position. No one would be wrong. No one would be right either. Each would simply have an opinion on a particular subject or situation. This would allow open and honest communication and exploration into each other's positions. This lack of defense allows people to build trust, even if they hold extremely different opinions.

Eventually we can understand that both parties are in fact right, since each person's position is correct (right) for them at that time. We need to understand that having different beliefs gives us an opportunity to love each other and ourselves. If we all believed in the same things, we wouldn't judge one another, and there would be no opportunity to practice letting go of our judgments. Allowing others to hold a strikingly different opinion while still seeing them as your savior has a far greater healing effect on the planet than siding with those whose beliefs are compatible with your own.

It all starts with **you**. Never underestimate the power that you have in changing the world. The first and foremost step is recognizing that each and every person is our savior: my husband, my mother, my father, my children, my friends, my boss, my minister, my president, the panhandler I pass on the way to work. All are my savior. You are the savior of the world. Can you accept that role for yourself?

Exercises

1. Choose today to see people as your savior. While
    walking down the street or riding the bus, acknowl-
    edge the passerby as your savior. Choose to see and
    treat someone at work as your savior. Choose to see
    and treat someone at home as your savior. Record your
    feelings at the end of the each day. Do this for at least
    one week and notice the changes in yourself.

2. Practice the art of listening. Be totally focused on the
    person talking to you. Don't judge what they are
    saying or how they are saying it; simply practice being
    present for them. How does this feel? Did you notice
    any change in the person during the exchange or
    afterwards? Did you notice any change in yourself?

3. Sit or stand next to a person with whom you hold
    differing opinions. Discuss an issue. Now sit opposite
    one another. How does that feel different? Switch back
    to side-by-side and feel the difference. Practice this
    technique at work and at home and watch the magic
    that happens.

16

Your Purpose in Life

The following is guidance received during meditation.

"Let us make this perfectly clear. You are the Universal mind, whatever name you choose to call it: "Christ mind," "Universal intelligence." You are it. You are the limitless, unbounded energy of God. And this energy is conscious awareness. All this conscious awareness is aware of is the Truth of what you are. Do not try to find the exact words of what this means, because there are none.

"You do not open yourself to what you are, since you already are this awareness. You simply allow yourself to remember. You come to the point when this world, this life, this limited awareness, that you have defined yourself as being becomes meaningless. This meaninglessness can be quite frightening for a time. Let us assure you that this is a temporary stage, and is in fact important and meaningful within itself, for this starts your quest to find meaning in your life—your purpose. How many times have you asked, "What is my purpose?" Your only purpose is to remember the truth about yourself. That is all.

"Many create great dramas in order to acknowledge the meaninglessness in their lives. Others create these dramas so as not to remember; to stay preoccupied. But sooner or later everyone turns away from intense focus on the physical and asks this question, "Who am I?" and "What is my purpose?"

*"These are perennial and age old questions. Who am I? What is
my purpose? What is my function here? Let us make it very clear—
your function here is to extend love. You've read it many places
and heard it in many forms. A Course in Miracles explains that
your function is to extend love to your brothers and sisters and
yourself. When you feel "off" purpose, you have chosen not to extend this love, and you miss it and feel a void within yourself. The
questions of purpose, meaning, and function arise only because
you are not actively participating in this function. If you were
readily extending love, you would not feel the urge to ask such
questions.*

*"There is a tendency to put conditions on "loving." You often
think: I want someone to love me. This is the source of "romantic
love." You seek out this one person who will love you more than
anyone else, so you can finally feel love. This is backward. It is very
simple, and yet so many of you make it very complicated. All you
need to do is love. Extend love, not just to one special person but to
everyone, without exception. This is how you feel the kingdom of
heaven. It is through loving that you find yourself and your meaning in this life. It is through love that you live and fulfill your
purpose. It is through love that you 'come home.'*

*"Why do you insist on making it so very complicated? You search
for yourself in your work, in doing, in special love relationships,
but it will not be found there, unless your focus and primary purpose is to extend love. You are impatient, and yet the freedom you
seek is at your fingertips. All you need is to extend your love. It is
so simple—and even knowing that this is your salvation, you insist on putting conditions upon those you would love. You find
fault, you make excuses. What are you doing? Quite obviously,
you are withholding love from yourself, because you still feel a need
to be separate, because in fact you still feel inferior. You need not.
Love is what you are, the glorious love of God. And God does not
put conditions on His/Her love. God can't.*

*"God is absolute, complete, and quite frankly hard to put into
words. Do not look for your purpose. Extend love. The more you
do this, the more love you will feel, the more you feel, the more you*

*will understand that **feeling the love of God** is what you are about. You will once again feel worthy to feel and Be as you were created."*

This message is not about the words. It is the feeling I receive while I write the message. It is the knowing between the words that brings me peace and understanding. The absolute Truth lies in the space between the words. Words can be read, heard, used as affirmations, and they can continue to be meaningless. You can say one thing and feel something entirely different at the same time. I must listen between the words for the feeling.

17

What is the Truth?

So what is the Truth? The Truth on this plane of existence is difficult to understand, because everyone's truth is based upon their needs, their programming, and their individual perceptions. My understanding of truth has been changing for as long as I can remember. It continues to change even as I write this book.

As I shared in the beginning of this book, the initial stages of my remembering process involved developing a new perception of God. I was taught to believe in a fear-inspiring God—a father figure who would punish me if I did not abide by the rules of the Church. I was damned eternally to hell if I missed mass on Sunday or ate meat on Friday. Today I cannot imagine believing in such a concept. My God is a God of absolute love, a force that neither judges nor condemns. I no longer believe in a God that tests me. My Higher Power does not send me quizzes to see how well I am progressing along my spiritual path. My God sees me as I was created: whole, complete, and perfect.

In the section "About God" at the beginning of the book, I asked you to suspend your beliefs or judgments about God. Let me now ask you some questions about what you believe. First, do you believe that God is love? Second, do you believe that God is absolute? Third, do you believe that God is perfect? Fourth, do you believe you were created by God, in God's image and likeness? If you believe that God is perfect, absolute love and that we are indeed created in this image, that makes **us** perfect, absolute love, doesn't it? After all, could a perfect God create imperfectly?

Perhaps what we have done is create a God in the image and likeness of man. We projected human qualities onto God, and we expected God to treat us as we treat each other. No wonder we have lived in fear of God! But in reality, aren't we the ones who choose to live in fear, and aren't we the ones who continue to punish ourselves and others?

We have discussed concepts and ideas throughout this book. We have observed how we play the game of victim, judge, and jury, in various stories and practical examples. We now understand that we focus on guilt and pain, thereby continuing the game of separation, through judging, blaming, labeling and projecting. This understanding assists us in acknowledging the Truth of who we are, in moving beyond our fears and pain, remembering that we are whole and complete expressions of love, joy, and peace.

I believe this about each one of us, without exception. We are the perfect extension of this energy of absolute love. This is my truth. We simply have forgotten this fact, and instead have chosen to pretend that we are not like our True Selves. We play the roles of victim and villain, and we project feelings of imperfection onto those around us: family, husband, wife, friends, business associates, political leaders, criminals, and even God.

How do we remember the truth? We recognize that we have become creatures of habit, and that most of our habits are destructive. We are accustomed to living in pain, be it physical, emotional, mental, or spiritual. We perpetuate this pain punishing ourselves and others for perceived sins. But what we are really feeling is separation from our Source. We believe that we somehow abandoned our creator (remember the metaphor), and fear that we will be punished by this creator. We believe that if we somehow mitigate the punishment of God (by punishing ourselves), we will not be so severely reprimanded by this creator when we return to our original "home."

Think about it. It is ridiculous to believe that a perfect God of absolute love would ever think of punishing us, God's perfect creation. But still we play out this insane drama.

We need to observe ourselves and each other, and how we continue to create this pain in our lives. What habits destroy our sense of worthiness and inner peace? What games project guilt rather than extend love? By examining the motives behind our behavior patterns, we can change them. Remember, the purpose of this book is to identify and remove our blocks to love's awareness. Every theme in this book assists in this process. By writing this book, I have continued to discover and remove the blocks that keep me from my truth.

I was gifted with identifying one of my blocks and receiving one of the most profound releases I have ever experienced, after completing the third draft of this book. Patrick and I were among 80,000 people attending a national convention. After one of the evening events, buses were waiting to take us back to the convention center. We quickly reached the parking lot and got in line for what we thought was our particular bus. As we were about to board the bus, however, we discovered that we were waiting in the wrong line and that all the buses to our destination were full. These buses left, leaving us standing in the parking lot. I was filled with anxiety and fear. It was much more than a "normal" reaction to the situation. I became more and more agitated as buses filled and left without me. Patrick was embarrassed by my behavior, which only exaggerated my anxiety to the point of terror.

When we finally boarded a bus, I asked my Higher Power for help in understanding my reaction. Clearly, I was upset about something other than missing the first series of buses. I realized that I often panic when I am in gridlock traffic, or when I get lost while driving to a specific destination. In this instance, I thought, "How am I going to get home?"

In Chapter Ten I shared that I was extremely afraid of my father when I was a child. There were many reasons for this. One occurred when I was ten. I recall my father driving down a four-lane highway under the influence of a substantial amount of alcohol. My mother suddenly grabbed the steering wheel and simultaneously put her foot on the brake, screaming, "Lew, you are going to kill us!" She told my brother, then two years old, and I to get out of the car and run, because my father "was going to kill us." My parents got out of the car while my brother and I ran down the street. Dad opened the trunk, took out a crowbar, and held it over his head as Mom, Ron and I ran down the street. My dad then got back in the car and sped away. After a while the three of us began walking to my aunt's house, which was relatively close to where we were. (Our home was over ten miles away.) We lost our way while walking to my aunt's, and it was dark when we finally arrived. We had been walking for many hours.

For the past several years I believed I had resolved this specific issue, because I have truly forgiven my father. When I remember this incident now I see him screaming for help, as he held the crowbar over his head. I may have forgiven my dad, but I had not forgiven myself. Often we are convinced that we have cleared a block, only to have it reappear again at a deeper level.

When Pat and I arrived at our lodging that night, I asked my Higher Power to be released from this fear once and for all. I asked what is it that I really fear, and I heard: *"You are afraid you will never get Home."* This realization hit me like a ton of bricks. I still feared that I would not find my way back from the tree house to God.

How could I move beyond this fear? Several ideas came to mind: forgive myself for leaving the awareness of Home; stop blaming myself for my crazy childhood; practice patience with myself and *know* that all is in Divine Order. When situations that we believed were healed come up again, it is easy to question the value of the healing process. It might have been tempting to play the victim by stating "Didn't I learn this already?" But I wasn't tempted to play victim this time. I was determined to heal the issue at the deepest level possible. I asked for support from the Universe to assist me in this healing.

The next day I called Paul, a dear friend who lived in the area. He invited Patrick and I over for dinner and a weekly spiritual get-together at his home the following week. He also shared his enthusiasm about Playback Theater, a group with whom he had recently become involved. He explained that someone in the audience would tell the group a story, and then the actors would portray the story. This often had a profound impact upon the person who shared the story, resulting in a very deep emotional healing. I inquired if anyone else from the theater company would be there, and if it would be possible to portray my story; Paul said that it might be a possibility.

There were forty people at the dinner the following week. Paul and his partner, Bobbie had decided to throw a pot-luck dinner and celebrate both the fourth of July and Paul's birthday, which was the following day. We ate dinner and chatted with other guests until 7:00 PM, when the meeting started. Bobbie opened with a meditation and then invited me up to the front of the room. She asked me to share my stories of the recent parking lot incident and the episode from my childhood. The entire company of Playback Theater was present for this party to celebrate Paul's birthday.

My first reaction was, "I can't tell this story in front of forty strangers. It's too heavy; it's too serious; it's Paul's birthday party!" That was my ego. But a peaceful voice inside of me said: "Pamela, you asked for release from this fear at the deepest level possible. This is your opportunity." So I went to the front of the room and told my story. We chose the actors to play my mother, brother and me. Paul played my father. It was a very moving experience. I felt a tremendous release in the area of my solar plexus after they completed. The man who portrayed my little brother asked if I felt complete, sensing that there was more I could release. He was right, and I agreed to do more. I really wanted this! He asked: "Do you want a different ending to the story?" I replied "Yes." He also suggested I play myself.

Before we played the scene again, my friend Cheryl said that she felt that I had taken on the shame for my entire family, and that I continued to carry the blame for all that had happened. I realized that this was true. I asked the woman playing my mother to tell me during the playback that it wasn't my fault. We played the scene again, and it was one of the most powerful experiences of my life. I heard and accepted that it was not my fault, and I was able to release all the shame. Paul, as my father, kept repeating "What have I done?" and he asked me to give him back the blame that I had been carrying all these years. I did. I felt whole and exhilarated and incredibly grateful. I felt an enormous opening in my heart. I felt complete.

Reflecting back upon this evening, I am impressed by how many of the ideas in this book were a part of this experience. I have been carrying the blame for my family, as well as blaming myself, for over 30 years. No wonder I experienced pain! That evening I released the sacrificial role I had been playing. I stopped blaming myself and let go of the victim role. I felt enormous gratitude, and the walls within my heart crumbled. I felt forgiveness for myself—I felt free. I experienced the world as a very safe place once again, and I definitely saw everyone in that room as my Savior.

When we left Paul's home, my friend Cheryl told me that this process was not finished. I looked at her; how could there be more? We left on the six-mile drive to our accommodations. As I mentioned, it was July 4th and traffic was congested. We came to our off ramp, which was closed. We drove on, and suddenly traffic slowed to a crawl. Three police cars were parked on the freeway blocking all lanes, and a motorcycle policeman was circling in front of us to stop traffic. There we were: stuck on a freeway with **nowhere** to go. This was a magnificent example of my Higher Power's sense of humor. I could have viewed it as a test, but I knew it was a gift. We moved after ten or fifteen minutes and traveled several miles before the next available exit. We were stuck three more times and it took one hour and thirty minutes to arrive at our lodgings. Not once during that time did I experience the slightest bit of panic. I saw the entire situation as highly amusing. I KNEW that I was healed. This situation was resolved, and the magnitude of the traffic tie-up simply assisted me in this understanding. The entire experience was truly a gift. I was willing to observe my behavior and my habits, and to uncover the feelings of terror behind my behavior.

As we expose our feelings of inferiority, our fears, our insecurities, we can deal with them and begin to remember our True Self—absolute love. As we face what Carl Jung calls our "dark side," we find that we are not as dark or evil as we believed. That which we feared was but a smoke screen hiding only happiness, joy, and peace.

I find myself being much kinder to myself and to others as I continue to expose hidden fears and old habit patterns. I experience a deeper and deeper sense of inner peace and joy as I continue to release old angry perceptions of myself and others. I open myself to feeling unconditional love for myself and others when I discard my old beliefs of not being good enough or needing to be perfect in every task I do. At the same time, my beliefs about Reality, the environment, and God continue to change. Life looks much simpler to me, and it is easier to live in a state of harmony. The more inner peace and joy I feel, the more I see it in my friends, family, and environment. My truth is changing almost on a daily basis. I am stripping away the layers of illusions that keep me from experiencing my perfect Self. As this veil becomes thinner and thinner, I am returning to an understanding of my true Self: a perfect, absolute, loving creation of God.

On a practical level, every area of my life is affected. The more I align with love, the more I love myself just as I am in this moment. I accept myself in my humanness. I accept my body the way it is, my feelings and emotions the way they are, my mind, my financial status, my career—all parts of my earthly life are perfect just the way they are. I stop judging and permit myself to change if I see the need. But trying to change before acceptance creates resistance, resistance creates persistence, putting me back in a pain-filled cycle. My acceptance (love) of myself the way I am has opened the door to having everything I ever wanted: a marriage, a wonderful relationship with my family, a beautiful home, a fulfilling career.

Most of all, I have a sense of deep inner peace. It is from this space of peace that I allow myself all the "goodies." Through loving myself, I am willing and able to attract my good. Through loving myself, I am permitting myself to experience abundance doing what I love to do. Through loving myself, I am allowing myself to finish this book. I have gotten out of my own way. I no longer need to punish myself by living a life based on fear and lack.

Lesson 38 in *A Course in Miracles* states *"There is nothing my holiness cannot do."*[1] This is true for all of us. There is nothing your holiness cannot do. You can have, do, be anything you want. It is within each one of us to be the Savior of the world. Each of us can heal our bodies, our emotions, our thoughts and those of others. *"There is nothing my holiness cannot do"* is an inclusive statement. It leaves nothing out.

For myself, I need to use the tools in this book: acceptance, forgiveness, gratitude, meditation, surrender. I need to create these habits, because the other habits were so deeply ingrained. I need to focus my attention on what I want, rather than what my perception tells me is in the world. This takes time, gentleness, patience, and above all a willingness to remember the Truth about myself and everyone else. It is a process. It is a journey. But we do not take the journey alone. Millions of us are dedicated to remembering the truth. Millions of us are willing to see the light in everyone. Millions of us are changing our minds about who and what we are. Millions of us are awakening to this glorious realization. It will not be a long journey. *A Course in Miracles* calls it a *"journey without distance to a goal that has never changed."*[2] It is up to you how long the journey seems.

We, you and I, will experience a most wondrous realization. We will remember the Truth about ourselves and each other, and in so doing we will experience Heaven on Earth. It is happening now. Some of you already experience it. Some of you experience it at times, and other times you step back into the illusion of pain and drama. Don't worry. We never left the garden. We will remember the Truth. One of the steps in this journey is to experience Heaven here and now. Please join with me in consciously remembering your own perfection. Be vigilant in your thoughts and actions. Always extend love. Forgive your brothers and sisters. See all actions as love, regardless of their appearance. Above all, accept yourself, right now, with all your personality traits, fears, judgments, as being okay.

One of my favorite songs is *I love myself the way I am* by Jai Josephs. Perhaps we see things about ourselves and the world that we want to change. It's okay. It is all in perfect order. Quite frankly, there is nothing you or I can do to stop the remembering process. God created us whole, and there is nothing we can do to change what God creates. Relax and accept this. Enjoy the ride, and choose to be happy. It is your birthright.

Bon voyage!

$\mathit{Bibliography}$

QUOTATIONS: CHAPTER

2. The End of Sacrifice

1. *A Course in Miracles* , (Tiburon, CA: Foundation for Inner Peace, 1976), Text, Chapter 26, p. 506.

2. Joseph Campbell, *The Power of Myth* (New York, NY: Doubleday, 1988), p. 45.

3. *A Course in Miracles*, op. cit., Text, Chapter 26, p. 506.

3. No Blame = No Pain

1. *A Course in Miracles*, op. cit., Text, Chapter 27, p. 536.

2. Paul Ferrini, *Love Without Conditions* (Santa Fe, NM: Heartways Press, 1994), p. 131–132.

3. Ibid., p. 160.

4. Thanksliving

1. Richard Bach, *Illusions: The Adventures of a Reluctant Messiah* (Creature Enterprises, Inc., 1977), p. 57.

2. *A Course in Miracles*, op. cit., Lesson 35, p. 53.

3. Ibid., Text, p. 537.

5. Victim, Victor, Vehicle: Stages along the Spiritual path

1. Joseph Campbell, op. cit.

2. *A Course in Miracles*, op. cit., Text. Chapter 8, p. 144.

3. Ibid., Text, Chapter 30, p. 584.

4. *Courage to Change,* (New York, NY. Al-Anon Family Group Headquarters, Inc. 1992), p. 11.

7. Man Plans and God Laughs

1. Paramahansa Yogananda, *Autobiography of a Yogi* (Los Angeles, CA: Self Realization Fellowship, 1946).
2. Paul Ferrini, op. cit., p. 136.
3. Ibid., p. 136–137.
4. *A Course in Miracles*, op. cit., Lesson 24, p. 36.
5. Ibid., p. 36.
6. Paul Ferrini, op. cit., p. 137.

8. Time Management

1. Deepak Chopra, *Unconditional Life* (New York, NY: Bantam, 1991), p. 214.
2. Ibid., p. 215.
3. Ibid., p. 237.
4. John Mundy, *On Course* (Monroe, NY: Interfaith Fellowship, Vol. V #19, issue 150, June 1993).
5. Ibid., p. 4.

9. Meditation

1. Deepak Chopra, op. cit., p. 159.

10. Be Free

1. Pamela Galadrial, *Light of the World,* Fellowship of the Heart recording, 1986.
2. Chuck C., *A New Pair of Glasses* (Irvine, CA: New-Look Publishing Company, 1984), p. 68.

12. Forgiveness a Key to Abundance

1. *A Course in Miracles*, op. cit., Lesson 46, p. 73. paragraph one.
2. Ibid., Text, Chapter 1, p. 11.
3. Ibid., Lesson 46, p. 73. paragraph two
4. John Gray, Ph.D., *What Your Mother Couldn't Tell You & Your Father Didn't Know* (New York, NY: Harper Collins 1994), p 420.

5. *Peace Pilgrim—Her Life and Work in Her Own Words, Compiled by Some of Her Friends.* (Santa Fe, New Mexico: an Ocean Tree Book, 1983), p. 16.

6. Bernie S. Siegel, M.D., *Love, Medicine and Miracles* (New York, NY: Harper and Row, 1986), p. 31.

7. Bernie S. Siegel, M.D., op. cit., p. 190.

8. Marsha Sinetar, *Do What You Love the Money Will Follow* (Mahwah, New Jersey: Paulist Press, 1987), p. 22.

13. Beyond Addiction

1. Charles L. Whitfield, M.D., *Co-dependence: Healing the Human Condition* (Deerfield Beach, FL: Health Communications, 1991), p. 321.

2. Jed Diamond, LCSW, *Looking for Love in All the Wrong Places* (New York, NY: Avon Books, 1988).

3. *A Course in Miracles*, op. cit., Text. Chapter 29. p. 573.

14. The World is a safe place

1. Joseph Campbell, op. cit., p. 5–6.

2. *A Course in Miracles*, op. cit., Lesson 12. p. 19.

3. Ibid., Lesson 13. p. 21.

4. Ibid., Lesson 14. p. 23.

5. Ibid., Text. Chapter 16. p. 318.

6. Richard Bach, op. cit.

7. Michael Talbot, *The Holographic Universe* (New York, NY: Harper Collins Publishers, Inc. 1991), p. 54.

8. *A Course in Miracles*, op. cit., Lesson 22, p. 33.

17. What is the Truth?

1. *A Course in Miracles*, op. cit., Lesson 38, p. 58.

2. Ibid., Text. Chapter 8. p. 139.

About the Cover

The painting on the cover entitled *In the Beginning* is by Dario Campanile. Everything in the life of this Roman-born artist has led him to this moment where technique is overpowered by vision, where he sees more deeply and can share more fully his view of reality.

At an early age, the artist departed on his voyage of discovery with visits to the studios of metaphysicist Giorgio de Chirico and surrealist Salvador Dali. He has taken their visions and transformed them into a vivid, mystical, yet recognizable world of his own. Like all great paintings, his ask questions as well as offer answers.

Like all truly original artists, Dario Campanile, now 47 and at the peak of his powers, defies easy classification. His large oils juxtaposing wild animals with women of surpassing beauty haunt the mind and imagination. His still lifes are so rich and vivid one is tempted to reach out and touch the peaches, the grapes. More than merely realistic, they transcend realism into a new dimension.

His works are in public and private collections of such celebrities as Valerie Harper and Carl Weathers, among others. Included among Dario's European collectors is a former Prime Minister of Italy. He has created four record covers for Lee Ritenour, and one for Herbie Hancock. Dario has participated in group and one-man shows in Rome, London, Paris, and Washington.

When Paramount Studios decided to update their logo, some 500 artists were interviewed. In the end, Dario was selected to create their new image, now seen on all of the studio's correspondence and publications.

We're confident you'll agree that once you have entered his world that never was, your perceptions of beauty will be forever changed.

For more information regarding Dario Campanile's works please contact him at:
200 Tamal Plaza, Studio 115, Corte Madera, CA 94925 or by FAX at 415-924-6213.

About the Illustrations

Margot Gresham created "Margarts"©, the bug characters, found at the beginning of every chapter. She resides in Northern Virginia, where she works as an office administrator for an environmental consulting firm. She currently markets a line of greeting cards featuring her Margarts© characters. She can be reached by E-Mail at 102513,162@compuserve.com, if you would like more information about Margarts©.

Order Form

NAME _____

ADDRESS _____

CITY _____ STATE _____ ZIP _____

PHONE _____

Books
We Never Left the Garden ($12.95)   _____

Book-on-Tape
We Never Left the Garden ($24.95)   (Due out July '96)   _____

Music
We Never Left the Garden (Cassette $10)   _____
(Due out July '96)

Light of the World (Cassette $10, Songbook $10)   _____

*A Course in Miracles, Volume I—Lessons and Text Set
 to Music* (Cassette $10, CD $14)   _____

A Course in Miracles, Volume II—Songs of Joy
(Cassette $10)   _____

A Course in Miracles Volumes I and II (Songbook $10 ea) _____

Shipping
$3.00 for first item, $.50 for each additional item.   _____

Add additional $1.50 for first class postage   _____

California residents please add 7.25% sales tax   _____

TOTAL   _____

Please send your order to:
> Fellowship of the Heart
> P.O. Box 612300
> South Lake Tahoe, CA 96152

For Credit Card Orders call: 1-800-879-4214
(Book Orders Only)

Please allow 2–3 weeks for delivery

About the Author

PAMELA GALADRIAL is a native of San Francisco, California and holds a BA in music from San Francisco State University. She is an ordained minister and the founder and spiritual leader of Fellowship of the Heart. Highly esteemed as an accomplished speaker, playshop facilitator and intuitive counselor, her insights have brought peace, joy and understanding to thousands of people throughout the United States and abroad. For over 15 years she has worked with groups and individual clients identifying and removing the blocks to love's awareness that people hold within their minds, thus allowing them to live a life of health, joy and abundance.

Pamela is a teacher and student of *A Course in Miracles*, a form of spiritual psychotherapy and also has an extensive background in working with 12-step groups and participants.

In addition, Pamela is a professional singer, actress and composer. After many years on the stage in musical theatre, including a successful one-woman show, she focused her attention on her spiritual beliefs. This led to the release of three albums: *Light of the World*, *A Course in Miracles—Lessons and Text set to Music, Volume 1*, and *A Course in Miracles, Songs of Joy, Volume 2*. In her playshops and talks she incorporates her musical talents and her delightful presence in a unique combination of words and music, speaking to the intellect with her timely message and to the heart with her songs.

When she is not touring, Pamela resides at Lake Tahoe, with her husband Patrick, her dog Julie and her cats Katisha and Pooh Bah, where she writes, teaches and counsels.

What others say about Pamela's music

"Pamela Galadrial adds a new dimension to the experience of *A Course in Miracles* through her unique musical composition and style."
—Gerald G. Jampolsky, M.D. and Diane V. Cirincione

"Pamela's music reminds me of God"
—Alan Cohen, author of *The Dragon Doesn't Live Here Anymore*

"A Course in Miracles—Lesson and Text set to Music is a lovely blending of the eternal truth of the Course and the eternally beautiful voice of Pamela Galadrial. The songs are inspiring and truly bring the listener one step closer to God."
—Beverly Hutchinson McNeff, President, Miracle Distribution Center

"Pamela's voice truly carries the sweet nectar of the Holy Spirit. Her music nurtures the listener's soul as it speaks for God."
—Susan Trout, Author of *To See Differently*

Order Form

NAME _____

ADDRESS _____

CITY _____ STATE _____ ZIP _____

PHONE _____

Books
We Never Left the Garden ($12.95)   _____

Book-on-Tape
We Never Left the Garden ($24.95)   (Due out July '96)   _____

Music
We Never Left the Garden (Cassette $10)   _____
(Due out July '96)

Light of the World (Cassette $10, Songbook $10)   _____

*A Course in Miracles, Volume I—Lessons and Text Set
 to Music* (Cassette $10, CD $14)   _____

A Course in Miracles, Volume II—Songs of Joy
(Cassette $10)   _____

A Course in Miracles Volumes I and II (Songbook $10 ea) _____

Shipping
$3.00 for first item, $.50 for each additional item.   _____

Add additional $1.50 for first class postage   _____

California residents please add 7.25% sales tax   _____

                                    TOTAL   _____

Please send your order to:
    Fellowship of the Heart
    P.O. Box 612300
    South Lake Tahoe, CA 96152

For Credit Card Orders call: 1-800-879-4214
(Book Orders Only)

Please allow 2–3 weeks for delivery